THE WILMINGTON SHIPYARD

THE WIMLMINGTON SHIPYARD

WELDING A FLEET FOR VICTORY IN WORLD WAR II

RALPH SCOTT

THE History PRESS

Published by The History Press
Charleston, SC 29403
www.historypress.net

Front cover: Drawing of Liberty ship.
Back cover: SS *Zebulon Baird Vance* at launch, December 6, 1941, the eve of the attack on Pearl Harbor.

First published 2007

Manufactured in the United States

ISBN 978.1.59629.210.9

Library of Congress Cataloging-in-Publication Data

Scott, Ralph L.
The Wilmington Shipyard : welding a fleet for victory in World War II / Ralph L. Scott.
p. cm.
Includes bibliographical references and index.
ISBN 978-1-59629-210-9 (alk. paper)
1. North Carolina Shipbuilding Company--History. 2. Shipyards--North Carolina--Wilmington. 3. Shipbuilding industry--North Carolina--Wilmington--History--20th century. 4. World War, 1939-1945--North Carolina--Wilmington. 5. Wilmington (N.C.)--History--20th century. I. Title.
VM301.W56 2007
940.53'1--dc22
2007009409

This book is dedicated to
Nan Scott
Without whose assistance
It would not be possible

Contents

I.
Introduction of the Yard to Wilmington

January 1941 saw the resources of the British Empire strained to the utmost. War had been raging on the continent of Europe since September 1939. The moral and material resources of the island nation had been overwhelmed by the Nazi blitz, which had reached the western coast of France by the summer of 1941. Hitler controlled all the coast of Europe from the Arctic to the Mediterranean. Germany seemed on the verge of invading England the following spring and thereby plunging the West into what Churchill termed "another Dark Age." Britain's greatest ally, the United States, was forbidden by the Neutrality Act of November 1935 from sending vessels into the combat area, which covered sea approaches to England. The future of the island seemed bleak indeed.

The American president, Franklin Delano Roosevelt, searched for means to aid Britain. With his famously inventive political mind, Roosevelt did not take long to construct a bridge to England around the Neutrality Act. In September 1940, for an exchange of fifty destroyers, he received leases on western British hemisphere naval bases. Other forms of assistance followed. The United States could not yet become involved in the conflict, but preparation for war began under the guise of "the defense effort." An early "defense" priority became more merchant vessels. On January 3, 1941, the U.S. Maritime Commission[1] announced the first wave of an emergency shipbuilding program. Initially calling for sixty vessels to be built for the British Material Mission in the United States and two hundred for the U.S. Maritime Commission, the commission needed new shipyards; existing American shipbuilders had their hands full with regular naval construction orders.[2]

Factors that influenced the selection of the new shipbuilding yard locations were numerous: most significant were the adequacy of transportation systems and the availability of labor and management. Since World War I, Roosevelt had "been enthusiastic for shipyards in the South," to aid development of the area. The South, however, lacked many of the "white collar brains" needed for large ship construction activities. The South was handicapped by the "absence of mills making ship plates and by the scarcity of machine shops," although the area did "possess adequate supplies of lumber and certain iron and steel materials." On the positive side, the South had a favorable climate and was relatively well protected from potential enemy attack. Finally, large numbers of unskilled workers, low competition with other war industries and the need for reducing unemployment contributed to the decision to select the South as the location for a number of new shipyards.

These arguments, backed by White House support, convinced the Maritime Commission members to gamble on the South. Mobile, New Orleans, Houston and Baltimore appeared on a list of "well situated" sites for yard location. It seemed that North Carolina Governor J. Melville Broughton and developer interests at Morehead City, North Carolina, had an early ear with the Maritime Commission. However, when Newport News Shipbuilding and Dry Dock Company advocated developing a yard at Wilmington, the location of the yard ceased to be a debatable matter. Much to the disappointment of the Morehead City supporters, the Wilmington location was approved by the president. Wilmington, North Carolina, was destined to play an important role in World War II.[3]

Wilmington, North Carolina, possessed a long history of shipbuilding. The Spanish, legend has it, were the first European boat builders on Cape Fear, sometime around the year 1526. The first vessel of any size constructed by the English in the Wilmington area was the *First Adventure*, a small sloop of ten tons, built in 1727. Owned by one Michael Dyer, the first-known Wilmington shipyard dated from 1737, three years prior to the establishment of the city, but there were few vessels built in the area before 1800. The largest was the brigantine *Rebecca* of 128 tons burden, built by James Wimble.

In 1807 a number of navy ships were built as gunboats. These vessels saw service in North Carolina waters during the War of 1812. During the remainder of the nineteenth century, Wilmington continued its development as a shipbuilding center—Wilmington had two yards employing some forty-five hands. Most vessels constructed were small schooners for use in the coastal trade. A number of steamboats were also built in Wilmington during the nineteenth century, the first of which was the *Walker*, launched in 1831. Wilmington prospered as a shipbuilding center during the latter two decades of the nineteenth century.

The conversion of ship construction from wood to iron and then to steel had a detrimental effect on Wilmington's shipbuilding industry, causing it to decline during the early years of the twentieth century. World War I, however, provided a general stimulus to the shipbuilding industry in the United States. Wilmington obtained several yards under contract with the U.S. Emergency Fleet Corporation: a large yard for steel cargo vessels, a concrete steamer shipyard and two wooden shipyards. The largest of these, the Carolina Shipbuilding Company, was founded by New York skyscraper magnate George A. Fuller. The first vessel built in Fuller's yard was the *Cranford* launched in September 1919. The Carolina Shipbuilding Corporation built ten 417-foot, 10,000-ton steel cargo vessels for the Emergency Fleet Corporation. All were completed after the armistice was signed—all as Emergency Fleet Corporation vessels—never to enter a combat zone. Wilmington's World War I shipbuilding industry at its peak employed over four thousand shipbuilders.

Ship construction both in Wilmington and the United States generally collapsed after the war. The people of Wilmington had hoped that the yards would be permanent; however, this was not to be the case. Facing a closing of shipbuilding facilities, a delegation was sent to Washington to persuade the Shipping Board to continue the yards, but the group met with failure. The end of the war and the Depression of the thirties brought industrial activity at Wilmington, including shipbuilding, to a standstill. World War II changed this.

The earliest interest in a post-Depression yard in Wilmington dates from October 1939, one month after war broke out in Europe. On the thirty-first of that month, Thomas F. Little, a North Carolina promoter, wrote to North Carolina Senator Josiah F. Bailey concerning the establishing of a yard in the state. Little was initially interested in obtaining the contract for a U.S. Maritime Commission yard at Norfolk, Virginia. Associated with the Virginia Bridge Company, he wanted to use the steel fabrication facilities of the Virginia Bridge plant at Norfolk to construct steel cargo vessels for the Maritime Commission. Senator Bailey, as chairman of the powerful Senate Committee on Commerce, had championed the cause of the U.S. Merchant Marine and has been called the "father of the Merchant Marine Act of 1939." Bailey developed a strong relationship with the head of the Maritime Commission, Admiral Emory Scott Land, as a result of Bailey's chairmanship of the Senate Committee on Commerce. Bailey informed Land in transmitting Little's letter: "I owe to a sense of my own incompetence to pass upon matters of this sort and I must trust to you for your usual straightforward and candid advice."[4]

Little kept up his efforts. He came up with the idea of adding a branch of his proposed yard at Wilmington, catching the interest of Bailey, who it was hoped would in turn enlist the aid of Admiral Land. Little wrote, "Our State has nothing in the way of a shipbuilding industry at the present time and I should like very much to get back into the marine contracting field with a yard here, connected with the one now rapidly maturing in Norfolk." Little at this stage apparently received no encouragement from Bailey. Little tried applying a little local North Carolina pressure on the senator. On November 23, 1939, he wrote an open letter to the editor of the *Charlotte Observer* on the subject of a shipyard in North Carolina. Little praised Bailey for his efforts in reestablishing the U.S. Merchant Marine, but concluded by stating, "Up north they refer to Senator Bailey in marine circles as 'the Father of the Merchant Marine Act of 1939' while down here most of us wonder what the hell he's doing up in Washington to earn his pay…I suggest that you use your good medium to focus attention upon the need for a shipbuilding industry in the state."[5]

Wilmington interests also wondered about Bailey's lobbying to get a new shipyard for Wilmington.[6] Several citizens wrote Bailey expressing interest in a yard at Wilmington. As with Little's efforts, Bailey was not very encouraging at first. In a letter to Mr. Thomas H. Wright, Bailey wrote:

> *If an opportunity shall be presented, to obtain a shipbuilding plant at Wilmington, I shall be happy to embrace it. However, at the present time, the building of Government plants is not in contemplation and it is proposed that we shall use all our existing plants to the full extent. Should these be exhausted, then to be sure the Government will build plants, but since this will cause great delay, the Government is hoping to use plants already available. You may trust me to keep Wilmington in mind.*[7]

On June 24, 1940, the newly formed Shipyard for Wilmington Committee met. The committee authorized James Wade, Wilmington commissioner of public works, to go to Washington to lobby for a yard. Wade was accompanied by the chairman of the shipyard committee, and the group arrived in Washington on June 27 to begin their quest. They conferred at length with Josiah Bailey. The senator stated that most of the new construction was done in existing yards as he had written earlier. If, however, the group could raise a large sum of money, perhaps the Reconstruction Finance Corporation would grant them a loan and the Maritime Commission also might award the group a contract. It was all very problematic at this point, however, as Bailey emphasized that in the long run, whether North Carolina got a commission yard depended on the course of "the present conflict" (i.e., events in Europe). If the expanding European conflict dictated demand for more vessels, he would be in a better position to help the Wilmington group obtain a new yard.[8]

The group then went to the American Municipal Association, where they spoke with Richard H. Owsley and Earl Mallery, Washington representative and director, respectively, of the American Municipal Association. The two men pledged their assistance. Wade then went to see John Carmody of the Federal Works Agency. Carmody was out of town, but Wade was sent to Perry A. Fellow, acting commissioner of the Work Progress Administration, only to learn that the WPA was currently interested primarily in expansion of airports and military air facilities.[9]

Wade then approached the Maritime Commission. Admiral Land was out, but Howard L. Vickery, vice-chairman of the Maritime Commission, spoke at length with the Wilmington delegation. Vickery outlined the Maritime Commission building program and informed them that privately owned facilities were more than ample to care for the present needs of the commission. Vickery, however, reinforced the impression Bailey had given when he stated that "anything could happen" with the European situation. In the event that "the claims of Wilmington for a shipyard would immediately come closer to realization," Wade then approached the Reconstruction Finance Corporation (RFC). The RFC offered half of the matching funds to the Wilmington group if they had title to the land, had secured a contract from the Maritime Commission and had raised the other half of the capital as collateral. Thus fortified with the rather meek offers of aid from the Washington groups, the Wilmington representatives returned home. Bailey and Robert Reynolds, the other senator from North Carolina, wrote letters pledging to keep the Wilmington group in mind if any new contracts surfaced in Washington.[10]

In September of 1940, Bailey received a letter from Dr. Benjamin F. Royal, a local dentist and chairperson of the Morehead City Port Commission, announcing that one Thomas F. Little had approached a group in the Morehead City area concerning a shipyard. Bailey replied that Little had "been trying to get something done in the shipbuilding line for some months." Bailey questioned whether Little could be interested in both Norfolk and Morehead, but he failed to mention Little's interest in Wilmington. In a letter to Stanley Woodland, ports commission member, at Morehead City, Bailey stated: "I do not regard Mr. Little's first proposition as a reasonable one and it seems to me that he has for a period of two years been trying to get the government to build a shipyard for him."[11]

On October 5, 1940, Bailey wrote two letters, one to Admiral Land, the other to Secretary of the Navy Franklin W. Knox, transmitting briefs of a proposal by the "North Carolina Shipbuilding and Engineering Corporation" for a shipyard at Morehead City. Land responded three days later that he was familiar with the plan of Mr. Little, and added, "The principal change in the present presentation is the fact that Mr. Little now proposes to return his project to Morehead City rather than at Norfolk, thus going back to the position he originally took when the matter was first presented to the Maritime Commission some years ago." He further explained that the matter had been fully discussed with Little and that there was really nothing the Maritime Commission could do. Land concluded by stating that while he was not a prophet he had doubts as to the ability of existing yards to continue "after the emergency is over," hence the reluctance of the Maritime Commission to build new yards.[12]

Thus the forces at Wilmington were still empty-handed. Louis Moore of the Wilmington Chamber of Commerce wrote to the Norman Lombard Company, a New York construction firm, that Wilmington had been the site of a number of successful World War I yards. Lombard had written the chamber inquiring about the possibility of securing a site "for assembling welded ships" in Wilmington. Moore stated that Lombard's letter would be forwarded to one Thomas H. Wright, "one of our prominent businessmen," who owned the old Liberty shipyard. In the letter to Lombard, Moore cited the advantages of Wilmington as a shipyard site.[13] These advantages were later repeated by the North Carolina Shipbuilding Company and the Maritime Commission. Among the advantages given were ample supplies of fresh water and labor, considerable amount of space available with room for expansion, adequate rail links and a mild climate to allow for outdoor erection of subassemblies.[14]

Perhaps the most important fact that led to the eventual location of North Carolina Shipbuilding Company in Wilmington was the proximity of the site to the parent company in Newport News, Virginia. The search by the Newport News Shipbuilding and Dry Dock Company for an additional East Coast site goes back to World War I.[15] At that time, Homer L. Ferguson, World War II president of the Newport News Company, conducted a survey of Atlantic and Gulf Coast ports for the U.S. Shipping Board looking for sites for additional yards. Ferguson's report to the board indicated that "in his judgment it [Wilmington] was the best place on the South Atlantic coast to build an additional shipyard."[16] His report led to the selection of the city during World War I as a site for two Shipping Board–directed yards.

Primarily as a result of the World War I yards, the New Hanover County Defense Council, at the instigation of Hugh MacRae, began to lobby with Newport News for a defense shipbuilding yard at Wilmington. Correspondence from MacRae to Homer L. Ferguson, president of Newport News Shipyard, dates from late 1940 on the matter.[17] Initially Newport News Shipbuilding was not interested in building another facility at Wilmington or anywhere else for that matter. Newport News had just undergone the painful 1930 Depression period in United States shipbuilding activity. As early as the mid-thirties, the Maritime Commission had begun to provide the "Big Five" U.S. shipbuilders (Newport News, Federal, New York, Sun and Bethlehem Shipbuilding Corporations) with construction contracts that would allow the yards to stay in business and at the same time renew the strength of the U.S. Merchant Marine. Increased naval (e.g., carrier *Yorktown*) and passenger vessel (e.g., USS *America*) construction had enabled the Newport News yard to emerge from the shadows of the Depression.

As the war spread in late 1940, the need for more vessels increased. American defense preparedness, together with additional orders for vessels to be used in the increasingly profitable war material trade to belligerents, caused Newport News officials to again review the need for a new company yard. They chose to construct these additional vessels in the existing company facilities in Virginia. Newport News officials felt that the war would still be short-lived and that there was little need for additional expansion. As 1940 wore on, the increasingly heavy naval construction squeezed out the Maritime Commission work in the Big Five yards.[18]

Homer Ferguson, a native of North Carolina, had long cherished the notion of locating a plant back in his home state. Economic conditions had prevented this, however, during the thirties. Now with increasing war contracts, a new plant might just be possible. An engineering survey party was sent to Wilmington by Ferguson in late December of 1940. The New Hanover Defense Council, a group of concerned local businessmen, appointed a special shipyard committee headed by Ronaldo B. Page. Other committee members were Bruce Cameron, Hugh MacRae, John Alexius and James Wade. This committee prepared extensive data on the Wilmington area for the survey party. In the end a number of new factors caused the plant to be located in Wilmington.[19]

The desire of the Newport News Shipbuilding Company to prevent the establishment of another nearby competitor played a major role in the Wilmington selection. Welding Shipyard and Bethlehem-Sparrows Point, both yards located on the Chesapeake, provided competition for Newport News Shipyard. The construction of another major yard at Wilmington by the Kaiser Corporation would serve only to increase the competition for scarce postwar business. Newport News Shipyard and Dry Dock Company could establish an offspring yard at Wilmington for the duration of the war, and then close it. This would supply the Maritime Commission war effort for ships, and the needs of local business groups for war jobs, and accompanying war "prosperity," yet allow the parent company later to close off competition. Also important in selecting Wilmington was the World War I survey by Ferguson that outlined the previously mentioned assets of the Wilmington and New Hanover areas.

The Maritime Commission's decision to back the yard in Wilmington as a subsidiary of the Newport News Company had a profound impact on eastern North Carolina. The high elected officials of the state favored Morehead City as a site for the yard. They were overruled in Washington by the Maritime Commission. The potential for orderly growth in the East by the construction of a permanent shipbuilding facility in a site selected by the state's elected officials was thus thwarted. The failure of these state officials to secure a permanent facility had a disastrous effect on both planning and postwar employment in North Carolina. The Maritime Commission projected a second wave of plant construction to handle the increased load. On the list of contemplated facilities was a request by the governor of North Carolina, J. Melville Broughton, and other political leaders in the Tarheel State for the mentioned plant at Morehead City, North Carolina.[20]

On November 11, 1940, Governor-elect J. Melville Broughton wrote a letter on behalf of the Morehead City group. He stated that Ben Royal, Cy Gibbs and Stanley Woodland of Morehead City had met with him and discussed the plan for a yard at Morehead. Broughton asked that the group be given aid in an upcoming visit to Washington to secure a shipyard contract. Broughton stated, "It is possible that some other city located in the coastal area may be making…some effort along a similar line. If so, of course, I would be equally interested in cooperating with them." Morehead forces, in short, were enlisting the new governor in their quest (or rather Mr. Little's quest) for a new yard. However, events at the Maritime Commission were soon to take a rather fatal turn for the Morehead City group.[21]

II.
The Decision to Establish the Yard

In early November 1940, the Maritime Commission decided to locate the yard at Wilmington. A memo from Admiral Emory Scott Land to William S. Knudsen, former executive president of General Motors and now President Roosevelt's director general of the Office of Production Management (OPM) on November 8, 1940, outlined the procedure for producing vessels in quantity for the Maritime Commission. Land enclosed a list of one hundred shipbuilding ways in fourteen project yards, compiled in order of priority. Site number twelve was listed as "Norfolk, Va., Wilmington, N.C., or Moorhead City [*sic*], N.C., 6–8 ways, 3 possible sites (use only one)."[22]

Another memo from Land to Knudsen five days later on November 13, 1940, stated that Land "had given further study to the matter of providing shipbuilding plants." Land included figures for the cost of land, shop and plant facilities based on the costs of the Hog Island plant. Land went on to state:

> *Serious consideration should be given the advisability of setting up 14 or more separate shipbuilding establishments, practically all new, in view of present conditions in the shipbuilding industry, against one or possibly two large plants on each coast and possibly one on the Gulf, when consideration is given existing shipbuilding loads in each general locality, the limited skilled labor that could be made available, the equipment especially machine tools that could be made available, the housing conditions, etc. Reducing the number of new plants to four or less reduces the overhead including the white collar engineers and supervisors, and generally the "know how" required. Results should be accomplished quicker with the minimum of additional shipyards, with less interference to existing yards on Naval and Maritime shipbuilding programs, especially in the scamping of labor.*

This memo listed four existing yards, two under contract for British ocean-class vessels, and eight new yards. The seventh new yard listed was Morehead City, North Carolina, but unfortunately for Morehead City's interests, its name was crossed out and the name of Wilmington penciled in. Around November 13, 1940, the interest in Morehead City met a fatal end at the Maritime Commission.[23]

Knudsen wrote to President Roosevelt: "In compliance with your instruction there is submitted the attached sheet outline 100 additional ways in fourteen possible locations." Wilmington was listed as the ninth new yard to be constructed. This time there were no penciled changes. Admiral Land relates in his autobiography,

> *My friendship with Homer Ferguson led to one of the best chores I ever accomplished for the Merchant Marine directly and the Navy indirectly, when I persuaded him to start a shipbuilding plant for cargo vessels at Wilmington, North Carolina with a nucleus of men and my Naval Academy football friend Captain Roger Williams, sent there from Newport News. This piece of business followed a happy and successful day with Homer in a duck blind at Hog Island.*

One can speculate that the information on the Hog Island yard contained in the November 13 memo to Knudsen was also obtained in the famous Hog Island duck blind. It appears that Land quickly lost interest in Morehead City after the talk with Ferguson. Josiah Bailey and J.M. Broughton, however, continued to remind Land of the Carteret County site.[24]

In December of 1940, Little again wrote to Bailey requesting funds for Morehead. Bailey forwarded the letter to Land. Land replied that he "was struck with the tenacity of Mr. Thomas F. Little on the subject of shipbuilding…I thoroughly enjoyed the dinner we had recently and the opportunity of talking with you." Both Bailey and Land again rejected the Little proposal for a yard at Morehead.[25]

Chairman of the Morehead City Port Commission Ben Royal and Little continued, however, to lobby for the yard at Morehead. Congressman Graham Barden and Harold D. Cooley received memorandums in late December of 1940 on the yard. A formal brief with yard plans was filed with the Maritime Commission and Senator Bailey. The proposal was listed as the one of the Carolina Shipbuilding Corporation. The shipyard project at Morehead City was started in 1938. Attempts were made "to obtain the necessary site for an assembly yard in Morehead but were thwarted by litigation over riparian rights started by adjacent property owner." For two years this property was tied up in the courts. The property title was cleared in December 1940, and could now be used for a shipbuilding assembly plant by Mr. Little and his associates.[26]

The new year, 1941, brought a frantic telegram from Little to Governor J. Melville Broughton. It read:

> *Honorable Daniel C. Roper tonight phoned Mr. Daniels concerning this threat to states interest in Morehead City and Port Commission is endeavoring reach you by phone regarding this urgent matter. The immediate intervention of yourself…is necessary to obtain consideration for the Port of Morehead…Congressman Barden and others are vigorously opposed to influx of Virginia shipyard labor…We beseech your vigorous action.*

The telegram is dated January 8, 1941, and was posted at Washington, D.C.[27]

On January 13, 1941, Homer Ferguson, president of Newport News, wrote Congressman Schuler O. Bland of Virginia:

In reply to your letter of January 10th, we would naturally have preferred to establish a subsidiary company in Virginia to build the hulls of the proposed cargo ships, but it seemed to us that Wilmington was the best site on account of housing and labor conditions and the necessity for speed.

By early January, the word was out that the Maritime Commission planned to locate the yard at Wilmington, North Carolina. The Morehead City group promptly increased their lobbying effort in Washington. In response to the keen disappointment of the Morehead City interests, Josiah Bailey wrote in a letter to Benjamin Royal:

I have at all times been favorable to getting a first class shipping activity for the Morehead-Beaufort waters. I still think matters will so turn out that there will be a first class activity off the deep water between Morehead and Beaufort and along side the railroad.

The Newport News Shipbuilding and Dry Dock Company selected Wilmington for reasons of its own…

I have nothing whatever against Mr. Thomas Little, but I think I owe it to you to say that he has not made a good impression at Washington so far as the Maritime Commission is concerned. He started out for a Virginia site, as you know, and was turned down. He became very persistent, but the more he pressed the less favor was gained. You will notice that he is regarded as a promoter.

On January 21, no one less than President Roosevelt wrote to Thomas Little in care of the Morehead City Port Commission

in order to select the best site with the proper requisites behind the site as outlined herein. It is my further understanding that your proposals have been and will be given full consideration by the Maritime Commission it is noted that your proposals relative to a shipyard in Morehead City have been taken up with the Navy Department. The Maritime Commission advises me that you have submitted a number of proposals during the past year at several different localities. With regard to the present emergency ship program to be undertaken by the Maritime Commission, you are advised that this Commission has announced as Requisites for consideration of shipbuilding proposals the following points:
(a) geographical location…
(b) shipbuilding brains…
(c) financial structure…
It is my understanding that consideration is being given to a shipbuilding site in North Carolina and that the Maritime Commission is investigating the various projects put forward Governmental Agencies concerned in connection with shipbuilding projects.

Josiah Bailey responded in a similar vein to J. Melville Broughton on January 23, 1941. Royal conferred with Governor Broughton on the matter of the Morehead yard. Royal wrote a memo describing the conference with Josiah Bailey. Little's stock was sinking fast with the Morehead City group. On January 29, Bailey wrote to Royal, "I have nothing against Mr. Little, but I have not yet found anything in his favor. His connection with the Charleston Shipbuilding Company, according to Bradstreet's report, was of a promoter. His whole difficulty is that he created a background here over a period of more than a year that was not favorable to him. He got nowhere with his Virginia proposition and then invaded Morehead." Little was destined to remain in the fray a while more, however. The Morehead City group continued its lobbying activity into the spring of 1941.[28]

On April 4, 1941, when the next wave of naval construction was authorized by Roosevelt, Bailey immediately telegraphed Royal in Morehead City. Bailey followed the telegram up with a letter to the chief of the navy bureau of ships requesting aid for Morehead. Nothing definite came of this latest venture, however. Correspondence continued to fly among Little, Broughton, Royal and Bailey over the hopes of Morehead. By August 3, Little had hopes of securing a housing construction contract at Jacksonville, North Carolina, at Camp Lejeune. He enlisted Broughton and Royal in this venture. Mid-August saw a break between the Carolina Shipbuilding Corporation and the Morehead City Port Commission as witnessed by a letter between Governor Broughton and Benjamin Royal. At this point the commission gave Little his send-off. Royal wrote a long letter to Little on August 13, 1941, under the signature of the Morehead City Port Commission:

> *This letter is to inform you, therefore, that the Port Commission of Morehead City wishes to thank you for all that you have done in trying to have a shipyard established here and to assure you that your efforts are appreciated, but to ask that you refrain in the future from representing the Morehead Port Commission.*

Royal wrote a similar letter in the same day to Josiah Bailey giving his notice of the port commission "withdrawing its support" from Little.[29]

The withdrawal of support by the port commission, however, did not stop the persistent Little. He enlisted the aid of Rear Admiral P.W. Foote (ret.), vice-president and director of highway safety for the Carolina Motor Club of Charlotte. Foote provided the Little venture with the "shipbuilding brains" the Maritime Commission wanted. Little continued to petition Secretary of the Navy Franklin W. Knox, Representatives Graham and Barden as well as Senator Bailey and Admiral Land. On September 17, Little again wrote Barden concerning a concrete vessel shipyard at Morehead City.[30]

Senator Bailey at this point spoke to his friend Admiral Land, as well as with Homer Ferguson regarding the concrete yard. Bailey wrote to the old group headed by Royal that the concrete barge plant would be their only hope now for a shipyard at Morehead. On the thirteenth, Royal responded at length to Bailey's letter. Royal by this time was tired of inaction: "I realize, Senator, that you are a busy man, but a reply to this letter is not a reply to an individual but to a goodly portion of North Carolina who just can't understand why even the Washington snail-pace has not eventually brought some result to the Morehead City shipyard problem." Bailey responded by stating that after Admiral Land had a conference with Homer Ferguson on the Morehead matter, Land did not encourage Bailey in the Morehead prospects for a steel shipyard. However, the concrete barge yard prospects were bright according to Admiral Land. Eventually, Governor Broughton came to Washington for a conference with President Roosevelt over the Morehead City matter. The conference occurred in November, but by this time Admiral Land was not encouraging in even a concrete barge yard for Morehead. Broughton protested Land's poor response in a letter to presidential aide, Marvin McIntyre, on November 6, 1941. The Morehead City forces were by now almost spent. Throughout the rest of November the Morehead City group continued to petition the Maritime Commission for any type of yard for the Port City.[31]

On December 9, 1941, Little again made his standard offer of his promotional services, this time to Josephus Daniels. Early January 1942 saw Broughton continue his efforts with Admiral Land via Senator Bailey with regard to the Morehead yard. Land rejected these new requests from Governor Broughton as he had done in the past. After long last, this time the Morehead City group gave up.[32]

III.
Development and Operation of the Yard

The North Carolina Shipbuilding Company facility was located on the east bank of the Cape Fear River some three miles south of the heart of Wilmington, North Carolina. Construction was started on developing the fifty-seven-acre site of flat maritime forest coastal plain terrain by the Cape Fear River on February 3, 1941. Ground for the new yard was broken by a group of contractors specially merged for the large undertaking. The North Carolina firms of V.P. Loftis of Charlotte and Orrell and Underwood of Wilmington were selected to construct the six shipways and associated buildings. Early work of the contractors consisted of dredging and filling 400,000 cubic yards of material to form the land for the yard. The fill was then graded and some 950 feet of steel bulkhead was installed along the shoreline to prevent erosion. This was followed by the laying of runways for the overhead cranes and the railway tracks for transportation of raw material and subassemblies. Next came the pilings for the shipways, construction of motor roads and the erection of the actual buildings and assembly shops. Finally the large subassembly transport cranes were installed.[33]

Within the short space of three months, construction had proceeded to the point where it was feasible to lay the keels for the first two vessels. This was accomplished without a hitch on May 22, 1941. The speed of erection of the yard was a tribute to the skill of the two firms as well as an expression of the rapidly apparent need for vessels to replace those sunk by the Axis in the North Atlantic. As the war continued in 1941, the need for more vessels increased. Continued American defense preparedness, together with additional orders from steamship lines for vessels to be used in the profitable war material trade, only increased the demand for vessels in United States yards.

As with most shipyards, the yard itself was never really finished. In most yards, once a way is completed, another new, more modern one is begun. This was also true at North Carolina Shipbuilding Company. By March 1943, some thirty-seven vessels had been authorized by the Maritime Commission to the North Carolina Shipbuilding Company. This necessitated the construction of three additional shipways, a pier, an expanded assembly shed and additional electric power, welding and tool facilities.[34]

Some twenty-seven additional acres of land were purchased by the Maritime Commission for the company. As was the common practice with commission yards, the actual title to the land was held by the Maritime Commission, which used its power of eminent domain to confiscate the land. The land was then leased to the company, which ran the yard at no fee for use in war work. Later, the land reverted back to the commission once the war was over and the yard on the property was no longer engaged in defense work.[35]

Not only did the Maritime Commission own the land, but it also paid for and owned all facilities erected on the site. The commission did not pay the shipyard for construction of the yard. Only subcontractors, in this case Loftis, Orell and Underwood, were paid for the actual work. The yards were built for the commission under a fixed price contract (i.e., the government paid a set price for the finished yard). Later on in the war, however, as construction material became scarcer and hence higher in price, the commission authorized some additional expenditures above the agreed-upon rate. The major incentive to complete the yard on the part of the prime contractor (in this case North Carolina Shipbuilding Company) then lay with the profits to be made on the vessels themselves rather than in the construction of the yards. This forced the shipbuilders to hurry along the subcontractors in their tasks. According to the Maritime Commission contract, North Carolina Shipbuilding Company was not allowed to make a profit on the construction of the yard. All profits were to come from the construction of the actual vessels in the Wilmington facility.[36]

While the commission yards were of various designs according to terrain and geographical location, all of the yards could be reduced to two main kinds, depending on the type of assembly line. The commission encouraged the development of yards in which the material followed a straight-line flow, either in a straight physical line or with a final right- or left-hand turn as the material was placed on the ways. The straight-line flow prevented the problems associated with traffic flow in those yards that did not follow this method. The principal yard that did not follow the straight-line flow method was Oregon Shipbuilding Company. There, material was carried from the plate storage area to the plate shop, then to the fabrication area, then back around the plate shop and plate storage area on to the ways. Needless to say, this created unnecessary traffic jams in the area of the plate shop and plate storage. To save the hassle, the commission favored a yard plan in which the material flowed in a continuous line from plate storage to the ways.[37]

The two types of straight-flow yards were appropriately called straight-line flow and straight-line-with-turning flow (or turning flow) yards. The former were used on those sites where considerable inland area was available for expansion or where geography or congestion prevented expansion along the water. The latter types were employed in areas where land was not available inland either because of other use (such as at the St. John's River Shipbuilding Company at Jacksonville, Florida) or geography did not permit expansion inland (as at Marin Shipbuilding Company at Sausalito, California).

The North Carolina Shipbuilding Company yard was built in the turning flow style. Initially, because of the fact that most of the steel fabrication for the yard was done at Newport News Shipbuilding and Dry Dock Company, little space was needed for a fabrication shop. This resulted in a yard that had a rather small subassembly and plate storage area located along the shore and some six shipways located at right angles to the shoreline. Initially, because the plates were fabricated in Newport News, Virginia, the small amount of storage space that was needed for plate shaping at the yard was

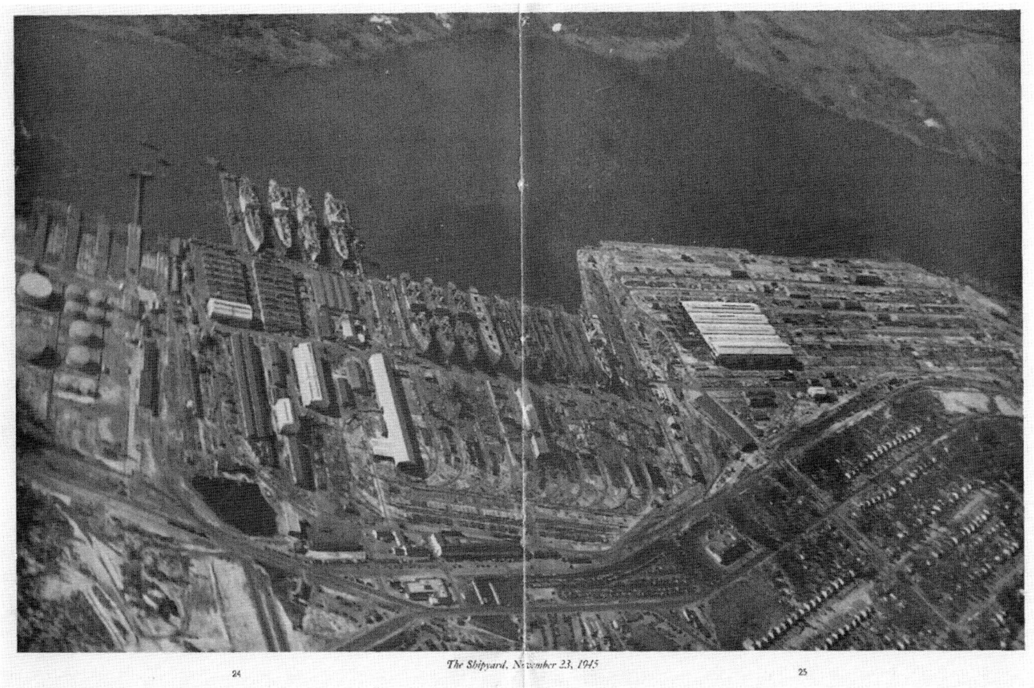

Plant Layout (aerial view).

limited to a small building, which was no bigger than a building way located behind way number five. In the summer of 1942, when the yard was expanded, the limited plate shaping facilities were no longer adequate and a more extensive fabrication and storage area was constructed to the north of the ways. Plate shaping done at Newport News allowed the yard to get by with considerably smaller plate storage facilities than were actually needed by a yard as large as the North Carolina Shipbuilding Company. The mild climate allowed for some assembly in the open, thereby reducing the need for additional buildings. The relatively small size of the onshore facilities at North Carolina Shipbuilding Company resulted from the fact that the plates were fabricated at the Newport News Shipbuilding and Dry Dock Company initially and that some of the work could be performed in the open.[38]

One of the innovative features of the North Carolina Shipbuilding Company yard was that large sections of the side shells of vessels were assembled on special frameworks outdoors. This procedure facilitated "rapid and sound welding" of these larger sections into the completed vessels. Other yards soon adopted this major assembly technique, as it was extremely practical. Most yards did not have the space or climate to allow for such large assemblies out of doors. These yards instead had special assembly areas for the prow and forepeak of the vessels. At the North Carolina Shipbuilding Company yard, however, this technique extended to the major side shells of the vessels. Larger capacity cranes were installed to move these heavy assemblies quickly to the ways.[39]

The use of innovative techniques such as these allowed the North Carolina Shipbuilding Company to build vessels with record-low man-hours and record-low total construction time. Other yards exceeded the North Carolina Shipbuilding Company times as special stunts, but no other yard maintained the record low times throughout the length of its contract. Climate and subassembly techniques provided speed in constructing ships, which led to the assignment to the North Carolina Shipbuilding Company of the contracts for the sorely needed C-2 vessels. Ultimately these fast assembly times were a vital factor in eventual Allied victory.[40]

In its mature stage, the yard consisted of nine shipways. The remainder of the yard was divided into two parts. To the north of the ways were the plate and shape storage areas and the plate fabrication shop. To the south of the ways there were three five-hundred-foot outfitting piers. A one-thousand-foot wharf was located adjacent to the storage and fabrication area. This particular scheme was highly functional because activities ancillary to actual ship construction (i.e., outfitting and plate fabrication) were conducted in two areas symmetrically divided on both sides of the shipways. Owing to the fact that the yard was located along the Cape Fear River, the layout was essentially linear. The depth of the property did not permit extensive construction at the head of each way. This necessitated a right-hand turn in the flow of material as it approached the ways. While this turn slowed the flow of material down some, it did not significantly retard the construction of vessels. The Society of Naval Architects and Marine Engineers suggest that the straight-line layout is the most efficient one for a shipyard. Due to the previously mentioned requirements, the North Carolina Shipbuilding Company yard was constructed in the straight-line-with-turning-flow layout.[41]

During the initial contract with the Maritime Commission the flow of material at the North Carolina Shipbuilding Company yard was in the following manner. The fabricated steel plates were received by rail from Newport News and stored in an outside area. Out of these plates, large subassemblies were fabricated in the open or in sheds at the end of the ways. These subassemblies were then carried by the large overhead cranes down the ways, where they were attached to the vessel under construction. When the vessel was launched, it was towed to the outfitting piers where the final machinery and joiner work was done. After outfitting the vessel then went on a sea trial down the Cape Fear River. After the sea trial, the vessel returned to the wharf for shakedown adjustments and final provisioning before being turned over to the contract holder.

After 1942, following the plant expansion, the above procedures were followed except that the plate fabrication no longer took place in Newport News. Instead, steel plates received by rail were first stored and then shaped in the fabrication shop at the area to the north of the ways.

The yard also contained an administration building, a cafeteria, a machine shop, a warehouse, an employment office, two outfitting buildings and two large indoor subassembly sheds. All this was connected together by nineteen miles of standard and marine railway tracks.

The shipways utilized eleven 15-ton whirley or portal cranes and nine 25-ton whirley or portal cranes. The large outdoor side assembly shed areas used two

SS *Zebulon Baird Vance* at launch, December 6, 1941, the eve of the attack on Pearl Harbor.

SS *Zebulon Baird Vance* floats free in Cape Fear River, December 6, 1941.

SS *Zebulon Baird Vance* being towed to outfitting pier, December 6, 1941.

SS *Zebulon Baird Vance* (hull number 1) prior to lauching December 6, 1941.

25-ton gantry cranes. The outfitting piers were equipped with two whirley or portal cranes of 25 tons each. Plates were moved to the assembly areas by a 10-ton gantry crane. The plate, shape, lumber and pipe storage areas jointly used the remaining seven 7½-ton gantry cranes for moving these materials. For smaller jobs, the yard used sixteen locomotive jib cranes and two tractor cranes.[42]

After the C-2 contract was let, a gear assembly building was added to the southeast of the machine shop. For security reasons this building is not shown on the plans of the yard, since the construction of the high-speed turbine gears was a top secret matter during most of the war.[43] This building housed the largest gantry crane used in the yard—seventy-five tons—and the building cost over $100,000 to construct. The largest gantry cranes were used where extremely heavy material, such as gear assemblies, were transported. This type of crane supported the weight of the object carried on two massive legs mounted on marine railway tracts. Portal or whirley cranes were used alongside the ways and at the outfitting piers because they could turn 360 degrees and thereby service vessels on both sides of the berth. For hauling heavy loads two Portal cranes could be run along parallel tracks. When this occurred, the famous "Bridge of Cranes"—a phenomenon typical of shipyard photographs—resulted.[44]

Even this vast amount of space and equipment along the banks of the Cape Fear River was, however, not enough for the North Carolina Shipbuilding Company. The company leased some 37,290 square feet of warehouse storage space in downtown Wilmington. The space was leased at the rate of seventeen cents per square foot for a total rent of $6,399.30 each year. North Carolina Shipbuilding Company certified to the Maritime Commission that the space would be used for excess storage, as there was insufficient space in the yard for either storage or construction of additional storage facilities. Since this was in 1941, presumably some of the space shortage was alleviated by the construction in 1942 of the new north plate storage yard.[45]

The rather extensive size of the shipyard created some unusual problems. Vessels traveling up and down the East Coast between Charleston, South Carolina, and Norfolk, Virginia, traverse one of the most dangerous stretches of ocean in the world. The shoal water of the North Carolina Coast extends far out into the Atlantic, making the passage fraught with tension and danger. This is especially true during wartime with the possibility of the presence of submarines. To avoid submarines, the coast-wise vessels hugged the coastline in an attempt at sailing in water that is too shallow for submarine operation. During most of the passage from Charleston to Norfolk, the ships merge into the landmass when viewed by submarines farther out to sea. The one exception in this passage occured when coastwise vessels transited the Wilmington area.

As the coastal steamers pass this area, instead of merging into the shadows of the land, the vessels are sharply contrasted with bright lights from the large metropolis of Wilmington. This unfortunately causes the vessel in passage to appear as a large target to any submarine operating to the seaward of it. In fact, several vessels were torpedoed during the war as they made their transit off the Wilmington coast. These unfortunate experiences led to vigorous efforts on the part of civilian defense authorities to reduce the amount of light coming from the city of Wilmington. The authorities found, however, that most of the light was coming from the large shipyard located to the south of the town rather than from the general populace of the area. This led to an interesting conflict between two war aims: shipbuilding and safe coastal shipping. The solution to the conflict was typical of wartime solutions to problems and even, one might say, grim realities.

The North Carolina Shipbuilding Company facility was illuminated at night 365 days a year according to a formula devised by Westinghouse Electric Company engineers for lighting a shipyard. The system used wide beam 1,500-watt light units mounted sixty feet above the ways for every twenty-thousand-square-foot area. Each of these areas generated some 330,000 total lamp lumens. There were up to 1,800 of the 1,500-watt floodlights used on the North Carolina Shipbuilding Company site. Together they generated some 60.3 million lumens, a rather major source of light in the area. A large portion of the light generated was reflected upward by the ground into the sky. When cloud cover was present (as indeed it sometimes is in the Wilmington area), most of the light reflected from the ground is displayed on the clouds. This increases the amount of light visible from offshore and served to increase the outline of passing coastal vessels during cloudy weather.[46]

In response to numerous complaints from passing ship captains, Colonel William S. Pritchard of the Internal Security District Number Two, Fort Bragg, made an inspection of the nighttime lighting of the North Carolina Shipbuilding Company yard on November 18, 1942. In his report, Pritchard remarked that while the yard did in fact generate considerable amounts of light, little could be done about it. He praised the company for its prudent lighting policy, given the wartime need for speedy ship assembly. He remarked that the floodlights had already been adjusted to face downward to cut down on the amount of light going up toward the sky. Pritchard also passed comment that the yard did not permit the use of exposed bulbs on the outfitting piers and vessels, as was the practice in most other Maritime Commission shipyards. Pritchard recommended the installation of metal shields over the lamps, thereby acting as visors to shield the light. However, since the metal to be used on the 1,800 floodlights was a critical material, it was felt that little would be done for the war effort if the metal were put to that use. The visors would aid in reducing the night glow but it would not eliminate it.[47]

Pritchard concluded, "If one weighs the importance of reducing the light on the work areas with the relatively minute quantity which such a procedure would reduce the sky glow, it is very questionable whether or not this would be advisable."[48] In other words, nothing could be done about the problem. The coastal vessels would just have to continue to take their chances. Of course, as the war wore on, the submarine menace became less and less of a direct threat on the Atlantic coast. William S. McMahon, assistant to the general manager, relates in a letter of December 10, 1942, to the Office of Civilian Defense in Charlotte, that the company received Pritchard's report and had "reduced objectionable sky glow as much as possible, considering the necessities of war industry production."[49]

This ending to a typical wartime conflict is rather interesting. The need for the shipyard to be illuminated for work twenty-four hours a day, seven days a week, had to be weighted against the need for shipping passing off the coast of North Carolina not to be illuminated by the yard lights. Eager to see that the yard continued constant work on the vessels, the North Carolina Shipbuilding Company provided the internal security agent with such transportation as needed for his visit. The company also provided Pritchard with a vessel with which to observe the sky glow from the ocean. Unfortunately, Pritchard stated that the "atmosphere was so clear that no sky glow could be observed from the plant."[50] In other words, there were no clouds to reflect the light from the shipyard. Pritchard also related, "A bright moon also was responsible for the decrease in visibility of sky glow since it reduced the contrast which would normally be present on a completely dark night."[51] The ideal night then to survey the sky glow problem would then be a moonless cloudy night. When did the inspector come? On a moonlit clear night, when most of the light from the shipyard went straight up into the atmosphere. Coincidence? Perhaps, but given the wartime demand for ships, this was a rather unlikely occurrence.[52]

Interestingly enough, when the yard itself was threatened, North Carolina Shipbuilding Company could react quickly. In the event of an air raid, all lights could be turned off at the yard within one minute. This successful performance on a test netted the yard permanent exemption from all regular New Hanover County practice blackouts. The workers could keep right on working with no time off for a safety practice blackout. However, should the facility actually be threatened by air attack, off went the lights. Unfortunately, sea captains were not afforded this instant means of protection.[53]

Having established the yard at Wilmington, North Carolina, the North Carolina Shipbuilding Company management moved on to solving some of the massive human problems attending the introduction of a large war material facility into a local community.

IV.
Wartime Shipyard
Wilmington during the War

World War II brought a shipbuilding boomtown atmosphere to the Wilmington area. The city became a latter day version of the Alaska gold rush as rural Southern farmers flocked to employment opportunities at the North Carolina Shipbuilding Company. Wilmington on the eve of World War II was a community much the same as it had been for the past fifty years. In many ways it portrayed the quiet slow prewar South. The *Federal Writers' Guide to North Carolina* described Wilmington as it was in the lazy late thirties:

> *The city, with a history of more than two centuries, is a region noted for the variety of its vegetation. The river is so thickly lined with piers and warehouses that it is visible only at street end and at the customhouse wharf. Fine old homes, many surrounded by informal gardens and some enclosed by high walls, are sheltered by oaks, maples and magnolias. Fountains and monuments mark many street intersections.*
>
> *White and Negro hucksters cry their wares in the early morning on residential streets and Negro stevedores sing work songs on the docks as they handle cotton, sugar and odorous fertilizer. Saturday brings a horde of farmers from outlying farms. The peal of many church bells breaks the Sunday calm.*[54]

Wilmington had not had as great a decline in economic activity during the Depression as the nation as a whole. In neither retail trade nor manufacturing did employment fall to the same degree as in the rest of the country. After 1933, the recovery was more rapid in Wilmington than it was in the rest of the nation.[55] The pace of Wilmington only really quickened with the coming of the North Carolina Shipbuilding Company yard. At its peak in 1943, the company employed more people than were working in all industries in Wilmington in 1940, including the Atlantic Coast Line Railroad. With its head office and shops in Wilmington, the railroad had long been the town's largest employer. Manufacturing expansion had remained fairly stable in the Wilmington area until the arrival of the North Carolina Shipbuilding Company. By September of 1943, some $310 million worth of contracts had been awarded to the North Carolina Shipbuilding Company for cargo vessels and to V.P. Loftis Company for floating dry docks. These two companies employed more than four-fifths of all manufacturing workers in New Hanover County. Where did the influx of workers come from, how were they trained and how did Wilmington cope with the large influx of populace?[56]

According to the 1940 U.S. census, there were 20,287 persons in the labor force in New Hanover County accounting for some 55 percent of the total county population. For Wilmington city around 30 percent of all female residents were in the labor force. These women made up 35 percent of the town's workforce. Unemployment in the Wilmington area was lower than the United States average, as unemployed masses from the Southeast flocked to the Wilmington industries. There was, however, a brief labor shortage in 1942. The local available labor supply was exhausted in early May of 1942, according to the U.S. Employment Service. The completion of construction work at nearby Camp Davis, however, added to the influx of laborers entering the labor pool in New Hanover County. There were some spot shortages early in the war effort, but by 1943 labor supplies, while not abundant, were at least adequate. The completion of Camp Davis and extensive in-migration of workers were responsible for producing an adequate supply for war labor manufacturing needs.[57]

Manufacturing employment in 1939 for the Wilmington area numbered 2,606 persons. By December of 1941, employment exceeded 7,000, as compared with around 3,000 in April of 1940. February of 1943 saw employment peak in the area of manufacturing at about 24,000. Practically all of this increase resulted from expansion at the North Carolina Shipbuilding Company yard. Wilmington was a desirable place to be in 1940, as compared with the more rural areas of the South. More than twice the number of income tax forms were filed in New Hanover County per 1,000 people than in North Carolina as a whole. In North Carolina, 36.1 persons filed returns per 1,000 population in 1940. In New Hanover County the figure was 76.6 persons, and for Wilmington it was 107.6 persons. The per pupil expenditure for public schools in 1940 was higher in New Hanover County ($41.75) than the rest of North Carolina ($36.41), but under the United States average ($76.35). New Hanover County had 6.1 hospital beds per 1,000 people as opposed to the U.S. Public Health Service minimum standards of 4.5 beds, and considerably better than the state average of 2.2 beds.[58]

In 1940 most of the houses in Wilmington were older than those in the rest of the county. A fourth of the building units in New Hanover County were built between 1930 and 1940, while only 5 percent fell in that range in the Wilmington city limits. Three-fifths of the houses in Wilmington were built prior to 1910. These units were in a better average state of repair and had less frequent overcrowding in 1940 than for the state as a whole. In October of 1942, however, the housing shortage in Wilmington stood at 3,000 units. By September 1943, some 1,700 permanent and over 4,000 mobile homes had been built to accommodate the influx of war workers.[59]

The permanent housing units constructed were of the following types: 200 dormitory units, 382 war apartment units (multi-family), 304 one-bedroom dwellings (single-family) units, 558 two-bedroom (single-family) units, 230 three-bedroom (single-family) units and 26 four-bedroom (single-family) dwelling units. The dormitory room rental rate was sixteen dollars per month. Some of these new housing units were considered substandard because they had coal stoves and because iceboxes rather than refrigerators were used. Some of the new units remained unoccupied because workers would rather take their chances elsewhere than live in the substandard units. These new units were constructed under a Maritime Commission emergency housing program for shipyard workers. All costs of construction were paid for by the federal government.[60]

In her wartime diary *Journey through Chaos*, Agnes Meyer described the Wilmington area during World War II. She states that the conditions in New Hanover County during 1943 were so bad that they made the proverbial long Washington, D.C., lines seem "like the land of milk and honey." When Meyer arrived in late April of that year, the five main food service establishments in Wilmington had used up all their ration points for the month and were "serving such odds and ends as they had left." Because there was little food to be had, lines were somewhat shorter than usual, Meyer relates. Even so, she waited for breakfast coffee some twenty minutes, and thirty minutes were required for lunch. Meyer abandoned dinner "because the meals were not worth the effort it takes to get them." Some local workers assured her that they often went hungry because of the small, poorly prepared food portions. New Wilmington cafeteria facilities were out of the question because a new owner could not obtain the ration coupons needed to get the food.[61]

A new well-equipped cafeteria had been completed in Wilmington but it was unable to open for lack of food. Meyer relates that the new facility had seating for 350 people, a solid copper dishwasher twelve feet long, surrounded by a forty-foot galvanized steel sink. The new facility had a "refrigerator large enough to hold all the meat that comes into Wilmington." In addition the facility had a twenty-foot stove, an "enormous oven," a six-foot-high potato peeler, two large dough mixers, eight-foot-high metal racks for drying towels and four stainless steel coffee urns. The new cafeteria also had fourteen stainless steel sinks, for what purpose no one knew. All this and no food was very upsetting to Meyer during a period of national shortages. She cites this cafeteria as an example of "the absurdity and inefficiency with which our war effort is being managed throughout the Nation."[62]

In contrast to this "chaos," Meyer found "the efficiency of private industry" in the example of the North Carolina Shipbuilding Company. The company was the most efficient producer of Liberty ships, producing vessels at "the lowest in dollar cost and second in man-hours per ship" in the nation. The company cafeteria was a case in point. The cafeteria was located just outside the fence between gates one and two. It had two dining rooms, one seating about five hundred white workers and a smaller one for blacks seating around one hundred. The cafeteria was open from 6:00 a.m. to 11:00 p.m. There were three serving lines handling some four thousand people per day. Fresh items were used in preference to canned foods when available. Meals were well balanced and priced lower than at cafeterias at other shipyards. A meal consisting of meat (usually non-rationed variety), two vegetables, roll and butter and a drink was served for forty cents. Many workers, however, stayed at their workstations and ate on the ground around the assembly sheds. Food was prepared in a central kitchen in the cafeteria building and placed on trucks and transported to small service wagons located at convenient areas. Some 8 percent of the meals served were done this way. The cafeteria was initially operated by the firm of Crotty Brothers. By late summer 1942, due to some complaints by workers of poorly prepared food, the cafeteria management was changed to the Raleigh-based firm of Warren Brothers. The main problems with the Crotty service revolved around unsanitary conditions, mainly flies and dirt on the floor of the cafeteria. Warren Brothers promised "improvements in meals, service and sanitary conditions." According to Meyer then, while "government inefficiency" forced her to go without food in Wilmington, the well-organized cafeteria run by North Carolina Shipbuilding Company served the shipyard workers a square meal.[63]

Since workers living in Wilmington faced housing shortages, many shipyard workers chose to live at home in the surrounding counties and commute to the yard. The commuter faced yet another shortage: transportation. In June of 1943 according to a transportation survey some 56 percent of the workers, or 11,852 people, resided within the Wilmington city limits. Around 3,700 persons or 16 percent lived more than twenty-five miles away from the yard, while 877, or 4 percent, traveled less than twenty-five miles to work. The resort beach communities along the coast (Wrightsville Beach, Carolina Beach, etc.) housed 2,367 workers, or some 12 percent of those employed. The most distant commuters (5 people) came from St. Pauls, North Carolina, every day, a round trip of ninety-five miles. Twenty-six employees traveled from Fairmont, North Carolina, a journey of eighty-five miles, and 40 came eighty-two miles from Lumberton, North Carolina. Some forty cars and eight trucks were used to move 349 workers to and from Whiteville, North Carolina. In total, some 4,395 cars were used by yard employees every day commuting to and from work. The company was forced to set aside a large area for parking facilities as a result. One hundred forty trucks and buses transported 1,639 workers to the yard. Thirteen percent, or 2,264 of the workers, walked from nearby housing units to the yard.[64]

The Maritime Commission obtained eleven large trailer buses and leased them to F.L. Formyduval to transport workers from Carolina Beach, Southport, Little River, Whiteville, Acme, Atkinson and Warsaw, North Carolina. These tractor-trailer type buses seated sixty people in the trailer section. Each bus was to make two round trips per day. The fare was ten cents and the buses were only for the use of shipyard workers and their families. Local Trailways and Wilmington city buses also brought a number of people into the yard. By March 1944, the Formyduval line was hauling fewer than five hundred people per day due to declining work in the yard. The Formyduval lease with the Maritime Commission was canceled on April 1, 1944, and "other operators… would serve the shipyard employees requirements." The few workers who continued to commute long distances continued to use Trailways and local Wilmington transit services until the last vessel was built. The commission noted on February 21, 1947, that Formyduval had performed his contract well and had returned all commission buses save one "destroyed by fire on January 20, 1943." The cost of the contract from December 6, 1942, to March 31, 1944 was $27,157.42.[65]

According to Roger Williams, president of North Carolina Shipbuilding Company, a great many of the workers were "off the farm and a large portion of absenteeism was caused by helping with the crops at critical times." The company approved of this practice and took pride in it because the workers were aiding two war industries: food production (and tobacco production) and shipbuilding. Percy F. Halsey, vice-president and general manager of North Carolina Shipbuilding, related to Agnes Meyer that the workers in the yard were of excellent quality because they came from neither large cities nor backward rural areas. Instead the laborers were "small townspeople or good farmers." Halsey related, "Last month 200 of them left to work their farms and the company shuts an eye if the men take off a couple of days to plant their crops." Workers who lived in the surrounding small towns had access to ampler food supplies than those who resided in Wilmington. The absentee rate was lower for North Carolina Shipbuilding Company during most of the year than the average for other Atlantic coast yards. The rate changed during the summer months, but no one cared.[66]

The number of workers in the yard grew from an initial "training cadre" sent down from Newport News in the spring of 1941 to over 20,000 by May of 1943. In 1943 the total gross payroll put some $52,390,140.05 into the county's economy, the peak year of the yard's operation. There was a constant need for more workers in the Wilmington area during 1942. The shortage at North Carolina Shipbuilding Company averaged around three thousand people per month that year. As selective service needs grew near the end of the war, the shortage increased. Declining Maritime Commission contracts and extensive in-migration to Wilmington saved the day for the company. The Wilmington labor shortage was in general not as great as in other war plant areas in the United States. An adequate labor supply was one of the reasons the Newport News Shipbuilding and Dry Dock Company located the shipyard in Wilmington in the first place. Where shortages did occur, blacks and women were recruited to fill the gaps.[67]

Some 30 percent or six thousand workers at the North Carolina Shipbuilding Company were black. Blacks were successfully trained as riveters, riggers, drillers, shipwrights, anglesmiths and other skilled jobs. Integrated crews were common at Newport News Shipbuilding and Dry Dock Company yards, and the practice was brought to North Carolina Shipbuilding Company by the yard management. Interestingly, while work facilities such as cafeterias and lockers were not integrated, work assignments were. While some tasks were relegated to black crews, still the majority of blacks worked side-by-side with whites according to their assigned task. This was in contrast to the other yards in the South that remained segregated. These and other yards used all black crews on one ship and all white crews on another. At North Carolina Shipbuilding Company the crews were integrated on most individual jobs, while some tasks were performed by all-black crews. The *North Carolina Shipbuilder*, the company newspaper had a separate column entitled "With Negro Shipbuilders," written by Thomas Jervay from October 1943 to February 1944. Jervay notes that the Harmony Kings, a black shipyard quartet, went to New York to appear on a radio program called the *Major Bowes Amateur Hour*, where they also cut some records in November of 1943. In July of 1943, the SS *John Merrick* (hull number 174) was launched. The *Merrick* was named for the head of the Black North Carolina Mutual Life Insurance Company, then one of the largest black-owned businesses in the world. The vessel was christened by Martha Donnell, Merrick's daughter. Blacks clearly played an important part in ship construction at the North Carolina Shipbuilding Company.[68]

Integrated work crews at North Carolina Shipbuilding Company shared similar conditions with other Maritime Commission yards. At Moore Dry Dock Company in Los Angeles, California, blacks were used mainly for clean-up, maintenance, rigging, welding, plate hanging and other heavy manual labor crafts. Blacks and whites worked side by side at numerous tasks in an apparently friendly relationship. Often, however, there was an undercurrent of traditional racial antagonism between black and white workers. William S. McMahon relates that he "expected a great bit of trouble" between blacks and whites at the North Carolina Shipbuilding Company yard. There were various "flare ups" of personal feelings at the yard. At Moore Dry Dock Company, in most of the whites "the hatred was basic, a deep seated and strong flavored aversion that was evident in almost every gesture or remark." At the North Carolina Shipbuilding Company yard, security officials would separate the races on their departure from the yard and force each race to leave by separate gates if they suspected that racial trouble was on the verge of breaking out.[69]

Katherine Archibald reported that whites were never wholly satisfied with the workmanship of a black. When the work was outstanding it earned the grudging admission, "Well, for a *igger, he's pretty good." The concept of black stereotype was reinforced in yard stories and comments. When a tool was lost or a lunchbox misplaced, often the comment was heard, "You can't lay a thing down any more with them *iggers around." It was the consensus of whites that blacks waited only for their supervisor to disappear to slouch down in a corner and go peacefully to sleep. Even when compelled to stay awake, blacks were supposed to have mastered the art of "doing nothing busily." One white worker standing around the yard was reported to have remarked, "Would you look at that lazy bastard of a *igger. Just hanging on the cable and pretending like he was really helping with it."[70]

The analogy between blacks and animals was frequently used in shipyard talk. Blacks were considered inferior, helpless beasts of burden. Archibald was riding home on the yard bus at Moore Dry Dock Company one day when a white coworker remarked on the unusual length of a passing black man's arm. "With those long arms," the worker remarked, "That *igger looks just like a chimpanzee." The worker added in serious afterthought, "They've found, you know, that apes and *iggers are very closely related." With attitudes such as these widespread on the yard, there is no wonder blacks and whites had to leave by separate gates in time of racial strife.[71]

This antagonism was largely the result of the blacks "trespassing" on what had been previously an exclusive white domain. As whites saw blacks move into the more skilled trades, the tensions increased. It was assumed that once a black entered a trade eventually other blacks would force all the whites out. Archibald remarked, "In spite of the negroes [*sic*] lack of skill and their extraordinary backwardness, they were assumed to possess some mysterious but potent faculty of evil which would hasten their triumph. Once again should the negro procure ever so slight a share in the white man's world, he would ultimately deprive its rightful owners of the whole." The admission of blacks, it was felt, only served to depress the value of the white man's labor in the marketplace. Soon there would be work available fit only for blacks. This racial strife led soon to conflict on the labor-relations front between blacks and whites.[72]

Initially, blacks were employed at Southern shipyards in a few skilled jobs; generally, however, the pattern was to assign blacks to inferior, heavy manual labor tasks. Blacks usually received less pay, training, opportunity for advancement and poorer working conditions than their white coworkers. Employers justified this discrimination on the basis of racial myths of black inferiority. Blacks, according to this theory, had high illiteracy rates, were prone to wander off the job, unable to adjust to industrial working conditions, had numerous "social" (i.e., sexual) diseases and exhibited general poor health according to the prevalent myth. In addition, the white supervisors felt that the black was ill-equipped, uninterested and incapable of acquiring advanced shipbuilding skills and education. Myths of black fear of work at heights or on water were common beliefs among supervisory personnel. A Mobile, Alabama shipyard operator complained that "it isn't traditional to hire negroes [*sic*]." while he commented that it was "impractical and utopian" to attempt to educate rural Southern blacks. Whites from the same area were strangely able to benefit by this instruction denied the blacks. In short, blacks were fit primarily in low-skill manual or janitorial functions. In 1938, in Florida, the Tampa Shipbuilding Company, under pressure from the all-white AFL Brotherhood of Boilermakers, Iron Shipbuilders and Helpers of America, signed a closed-shop agreement. Black applications for employment in the yard were denied by the union.[73]

The AFL attitude toward black workers in Southern shipyards is contrasted by that of the Industrial Union of Marine and Shipbuilding Workers of America (IUMSWA). The Industrial Union of Marine and Shipbuilding Workers of America first organized in the South at the Newport News Shipyard on April 12, 1935. While this attempt in Virginia ultimately failed, it set the stage for the IUMSWA attitude toward black workers. Van Gelder noted in a letter to Bath Ship organizer John Brown, that

> *one of the biggest problems there is the race problem, which you probably know something about… We are going to put them in the same Local and try to arrange it so there will be just enough separation in the meetings to satisfy the white men, and not enough to make the colored men feel they are being discriminated against. Of course we have got to work out some method of keeping them working together, or the ship will be sunk.*

This pattern of black discrimination soon spread by 1942 to most of the yards in the lower South.[74]

The pattern of black and white strife soon erupted into open warfare when in May of 1943, the Alabama Dry Dock yard became the scene of a pitched battle between the two races. Dodging falling "missiles and objects," blacks were on May 25 instructed by white workers to "get going *igger, this is our shipyard." A black man and woman were tossed into the river and several blacks were placed in shipyard lockers for their own "safety." Federal troops were dispatched the following day to restore order and enforce the resumption of the war effort. Eventually, through the offices of the Federal Fair Employment Practices Commission and the National Association for the Advancement of Colored People, the safety of blacks on company property was assured and additional skilled job classifications were open to blacks. This pattern of racial strife was generally not present in the yards of the upper South, including North Carolina, although it was a potential threat in the minds of all concerned.[75]

Integrated crews were common in the yards around the Chesapeake Bay region. Baltimore, Newport News and the Norfolk yards employed blacks, in the "normal" yard framework of seniority rules. Work assignments and on-the-job apprenticeship training was also available to both blacks and whites. When Federal Fair Employment Practices Commission Investigator Robert C. Weaver looked into conditions at Newport News Shipbuilding and Dry Dock Company in 1941, he found blacks working alongside whites in all areas. Weaver stated that the Ferguson shipyard had the "policy of not playing negroes and whites against each other." This somewhat enlightened policy toward the employment of blacks was in turn brought by the management of Newport News Shipbuilding and Dry Dock Company to the Wilmington yard of the North Carolina Shipbuilding Company. Unfortunately, this progressive policy toward blacks did not encompass company outlook toward union organization.[76]

At the peak of its size in September of 1943, the North Carolina Shipbuilding Company employed some 1,628 female workers. At the yard about one out of every hundred workers was a woman. The women generally had higher attendance rates than men. Women were noted by the letter "F" appearing preceding the employee number on their time cards. Fifteen yard departments employed women in their production work as welders, tack welders, burners, woodworking machine operators, tool checkers, tool grinders, messengers (riding bicycles), material checkers, chauffeurs, vulcanizing machine operators, band saw operators, metal checkers and drill press operators. Tasks performed by women included silver and "soft" (acid) core soldering, making gaskets, pipe threading and general electrical work.[77]

The first use of women in the yard was as tool checkers in the main tool room. The tools were checked in the room by the women and then filed under the "McCaskey" system of tool sorting. Women were next employed on a trial basis as welders. They became so good at welding that large numbers of women soon joined the main welding force. Two of this first group of women who entered the welding school on November 23, 1942, passed the difficult master welder's test of the American Bureau of Shipping. The women were Mrs. Edith Philips of Seagrove, North Carolina, and Mrs. Nell Rector of Wilmington. They both passed the test on December 10, 1942, about two weeks after having entered the welding school.[78]

The largest group of women was employed in the plumbing department. Here women produced the threading needed on the many pipes that went into the construction of the vessels. Securing suitable and safe clothing at a time when rationing of these materials was in effect was a problem for the women. Wool clothing, head coverings and shoes were special problem items. Wool could not be used because of the danger of welding sparks igniting it. A proper, safe wool substitute that was also warm for wearing outdoors, yet nonflammable, was simply not available during the war. Obtaining heavy work shoes in women's sizes proved a problem due to rationing of leather and non-availability of safety shoes in small sizes.[79]

Women had a special counselor, Mrs. Edna Cantwell, who supervised eleven matrons at the North Carolina Shipbuilding Company yard. Women were encouraged to visit with Mrs. Cantwell and to relate to her any problem they found in working in or living out of the yard. Women were provided forty-four separate restrooms; however, there were no showers or lockers provided. Women wore mostly slacks and tucked-in blouses. Few Rosie the Riveter–type coveralls were worn. Men's safety shoes or Boy Scout shoes were worn for safety by women. Most women ate at their workstations, on the ground in front of the assembly sheds. Sometimes there was dancing and special traveling entertainment provided by the company to improve staff morale on lunch hours.[80]

Women had equal rights in regard to training; there were no special classes for women workers. Women did, however, have a problem in the safety area. Due to the unavailability of safety shoes in small women's sizes, a number of them suffered from broken toes. Some women were lifting up to fifty-pound weights, with disastrous results when the weight was dropped on a foot. Until satisfactory shoes were obtained, the weight limit for women was lowered to thirty pounds in an attempt at cutting the injury rate. A safety clinic was held for two hours each week for workers. Even so, open-toed shoes and a lack of head coverings were often seen in the yard.[81]

A regular X-ray program was introduced into the yard in 1943. Workers were examined for signs of tuberculosis. The X-rays also served as an "assurance to women employees exposed to irritant fumes, particularly in welding." The exposed films were reviewed by a local doctor and then sent to the U.S. Public Health Service in Washington for a final examination. A ten-minute limit was set up for visits to the women's restrooms. The limit was "cheerfully accepted by the majority of women in the yard." Women found asleep in the restroom, if not sick, had their number taken down and reported to their supervisors. As might be expected given the working schedules, the women did not request a more active program of recreation. After hauling around fifty-pound weights, the women were no doubt too tired for a quick game of softball.[82] According to a report filed by the U.S. Women's Bureau of the Department of Labor the main difficulty with women was their "apparent inability to endure cold weather work" on the outside. Consequently, most women were transferred to indoor assembly jobs such as those in the plumbing department. Women were also indoors in the joiner shop, working with lathes and saws. The majority of these women were trained on the job but a few came with some woodworking experience. This was in keeping with the company's general policy of hiring unskilled workers and then training them in the Newport News system.[83] Undoubtedly some had experience in town or on the farm in cabinetmaking.

According to the Women's Bureau Report, married or unmarried women from twenty to thirty years of age without children made the "best employees." The company provided day-care facilities for women with children who worked on the first and second shifts. The report went on to state that the "few women that have been employed directly from farms and rural communities have proven more satisfactory than the average woman who has been a mill worker, cafe worker, etc."

Women worked only on the first (7:00 a.m. to 3:00 p.m.) and second (3:00 p.m. to 11:00 p.m.) shifts. No women were used on the third (11:00 p.m. to 7:00 a.m.) graveyard shift. Women were not allowed below decks to prevent the proverbial "hanky-panky" that was imagined could go on undercover. In fact, the company went to great lengths to preserve the reputation of its women employees. When a female nurse was first taken along on a trial vessel run, she was virtually locked in a cabin in the vessel for the duration of the run to Southport and back.[84]

Women were hired "with the understanding that they are to do a man's job and are to be treated the same as the men are treated. Each woman must carry on her work without favor and must do any work requested." The women were interviewed in a separate office in a building removed from the main hiring hall. "The applicant enters the front door, is given a number," which was called out by the interviewer in turn. After the interviewer talked with the women, they were either sent out a side door for a physical exam or sent home. This arrangement "eliminates the possibility of the applicant going back into the waiting room and discussing vacancies with 'undesirables.'"[85]

On the whole women at Wilmington performed extremely well during World War II. Change came fast during that period of national emergency. As recently as July 1941, a major shipbuilder did not accept women even as office secretaries. The firm had a lone telephone operator and as it was facetiously reported she was "kept under lock and key." By 1943 the situation had changed to where thousands of women were actively engaged in shipbuilding and repair work. In January 1944, over 10 percent of all shipyard workers were women. The need for women in the labor force was not realized early in the war effort. However, as male workers became scarce due to draft calls, women were pressed into shipbuilding roles with dispatch. In general, women's success in shipbuilding was a factor of the men's attitude toward women war workers. Yet often the women entered a yard before the psychological adjustment to their presence had taken place.[86] The needs of women were ministered to by the U.S. Women's Bureau.[87] The Women's Bureau stressed proper planning for the introduction of women into the shipyard. Yards were urged to secure the cooperation of male supervisors and employees, select and place women carefully, employ women only in "jobs found to be suitable" and to pay and upgrade women on the same basis as men. Women should have an effective employee counselor service and have access to the same training, food, study, safety and medical facilities as men according to the bureau. The Women's Bureau representatives made themselves felt by making periodic trips to shipyards to inspect and report on the conditions of women's employment.[88]

Primarily through the efforts of the Women's Bureau, the transition from an all-male yard to employing female war workers at North Carolina Shipbuilding Company was a smooth one. Women played an important role in the war effort. The use of women in the shipyards enabled the Selective Service system to meet their military quotas at the same time the Maritime Commission met their vessel quotas. Through the effective employment of blacks and women, the North Carolina Shipbuilding Company was able to maintain its labor force at its effective full strength.[89]

All workers at North Carolina Shipbuilding Company stressed safety. The company maintained a safety aid stock store in the yard where workers could purchase welding shields, goggles, mittens and other protective gear. North Carolina Shipbuilding Company had fifteen fatal work accidents during the five years of North Carolina Shipbuilding. Some eighty-one permanently disabling injuries were sustained in the company yard. In addition about 115,000 other injuries not of a permanent nature were reported in the five-year period.[90]

The accident rate of the North Carolina Shipbuilding Company was rather high. The frequency for 1943 was 62.57 compared to a national Maritime Commission average of 32.4, eye injuries accounted for about 50 percent of all injury cases. This was due primarily to a lack of enforcement of rules requiring welding employees to wear safety goggles. Large propane storage tanks and their vulnerability to air attack were also cited in a safety report. The tanks could not be buried, because of a high water table, so they were removed to a more remote location. Numerous other safety defects were reported at the yard. Lack of proper safety equipment and employees riding in material boxes up to the shipways was a frequent citation. The yard management attempted to improve the accident situation and generally they were successful in keeping fatalities to a minimum. Posters were placed in locked cases around the yard and movies on safety were shown to production employees. Having recruited their workers with some difficulty it was in the best interest of the company to see that the employees were able to remain on the job and not lose time due to work accidents.[91]

Having thus secured the services of its workers, the yard hoped that the employees would work safely and efficiently on the vessels needed for the war effort. Unfortunately, all the workers—including the blacks and women so carefully recruited—soon became embroiled in a long dispute over union representation at the yard.

V.
Labor Problems

In the period following the Great Depression, union activity increased in the American shipbuilding industry. In 1932, following a 15 percent wage reduction at the New York Shipbuilding Company yard in Camden, New Jersey, employees began organizing an independent non-company union to fight for higher wages and better working conditions. The movement quickly spread to some of the other Big Five Yards, and in September 1934, six of the local unions organized into the Industrial Union of Marine Shipbuilding Workers of America (IUMSWA) at a meeting at Quincy, Massachusetts. Congress of Industrial Organizations (CIO) affiliation was quickly secured, a move that benefited both groups. The CIO's increase in strength, however, only widened an already tense relationship between the American Federation of Labor (AFL) and the CIO.[92]

The early history of the IUMSWA was punctuated by strife both with rival unions and the shipbuilders. The AFL craft unions such as the International Brotherhood of Boiler Makers, Iron Shipbuilders and Helpers of America, as well as the CIO's United Federal Workers of America (which claimed control of the government navy yards) all hotly contested the gains of the IUMSWA. A New York strike in 1936–37 by the IUMSWA failed due to poor union organization. By 1938, however, the union had tightened control over its locals and membership had risen to over 100,000 members.[93]

The World War II era was the watershed of the IUMSWA organizing activity. Spurred on by the Maritime Commission, navy shipbuilding expansion programs and the Roosevelt administration's favorable pro-union stance (which resulted in the Wagner Act), the IUMSWA increased membership by 1945 to nearly 250,000 in some forty locals. Locals were on the East Coast, the Great Lakes, the Pacific and Gulf Coast states. Union organizers traveled widely to bring in new members from the four corners of the continent. As new Maritime Commission yards opened, IUMSWA organizers followed in short order. These organizers faced the same stiff opposition they met in the thirties, only this time from rival unions, company unions and the shipyards themselves. Throughout the nation the shipyards quickly became a second battle front in the war. The second battle was waged on the home front between unionist and non-unionist, shipyard worker and shipyard operator, black and white. The South proved no exception to the national pattern. In the South, however, both the pattern of anti-union sentiment among the general population and the racial mosaic compounded the IUMSWA organizing effort.[94]

Union activities in the South, modest at first, quickly increased as the pace of war construction grew. At both the Newport News facility and at the Wilmington, North

Carolina plant, the management followed an active anti-union policy. Attempts were made at both yards to introduce "company unions," as well as bar AFL-CIO members from working in the yards and other anti-union practices. This management policy largely reflected the attitudes of the workers in both areas. While the management did not stand alone in its anti-union stance (i.e., it had the support of the majority of the workers), the policy did result in the company being cited for unfair labor practices with the National Labor Relations Board (NLRB). Worker productivity, company profits and, in the end, the Maritime Commission ship output were hurt at a time when vessels were urgently needed for the overseas conflict.[95]

The formation at Newport News of the Peninsular Shipbuilding Association (PSA) and at Wilmington of the Cape Fear Shipbuilding Association (CFSA) in response to the AFL-CIO attempts at organization at the respective yards marked the beginning of a labor dispute between the two companies and organized labor that is still going on. As early as December 21, 1942, the North Carolina Shipbuilding Company was notified by the CIO on behalf of the IUMSWA that the maritime union claimed majority representation at the Wilmington yard. This marked the start of a labor dispute with the union that was not resolved until the yard agreed to a massive back pay settlement out of court. The issue snarled management and worker in the courts, and the dispute did not end until after the yard ceased production at the end of the war. The settlement for various alleged unfair labor practices amounted to $65,000 and resulted in the longest NLRB hearing in the board's history. Some 18,000 pages of testimony were taken in the NLRB5-C-1565 unfair labor practices case. The resulting labor strife deeply affected and divided the Wilmington community, and the discontent remained below the surface even after the war had ended and the yard had closed down. The story of the yard's relations with organized labor is a long and sad one for the people involved and for the war effort.[96]

One of the earliest recorded indications of union activity at the Wilmington yard is a substantial article in the IUMSWA organ, the *Shipyard Worker*, on August 28, 1942. The article, obviously written for distribution to North Carolina Shipbuilding Company workers, outlined the wage disparity between Wilmington pay rates and the union rate in IUMSWA yards. Headlines proclaimed, "Men in North Carolina yard lose up to $42 weekly." A department-by-department checkoff chronicled the union litany: "Anglesmith NCSB rate $47.60, IUMSWA rate $81.60," and painters received fifty-eight cents an hour at NCSB, while CIO yards paid $1.20, according to the *Shipyard Worker* article.[97] By September 1942, the IUMSWA had filed formal charges of unfair labor practices under the Wagner Act against the company.

North Carolina Shipbuilding Company was accused by the IUMSWA of dominating and sponsoring a company union, the Cape Fear Shipbuilders. The company denied the charges. In a letter to Percy F. Halsey, general manager of the North Carolina Shipbuilding Company, William M. Aicher, investigator for the NLRB, informed him of a "hearing to be held beginning October 15 (1942) at Wilmington, N.C. on the charges filed against the company by the IUMSWA." The IUMSWA contended in the hearing that both North Carolina Shipbuilding Company and Newport News Shipbuilding and Dry Dock Company had "by their officers, agents and employees formed, dominated and interfered with the operation of and administration of, and contributed financial and other support to, labor organizations among their employees known as the Peninsular Shipbuilding Association, and the Cape Fear Shipbuilders Association." The IUMSWA also charged that seven CIO members were dismissed because of their union activities at the Wilmington yard. The seven were listed as Joseph F. Blake, Harry White, Mack Reynolds, Howard McGirt, William Parker, James Scott and Solomon Hazel.[98]

The NLRB examiner had alleged in his formal complaint that the Wagner Act had been violated on seven different occasions at the North Carolina Shipbuilding Company yard. Specifically, North Carolina Shipbuilding Company officials had urged members to join the company Cape Fear Union, and had threatened to discharge members of the CIO. The company had in addition made "disparaging remarks" about the CIO union and had grilled employees on their CIO activities. Employees were also promised better working conditions if they withdrew from the CIO union and prospective employees were told that CIO men had been fired in the past. It was alleged that prior union activity was cause for non-employment.[99]

Coverage of the hearings in a local weekly newspaper, the *Wilmington Post* was somewhat sparse. The paper was largely pro–North Carolina Shipbuilding Company and anti-union. The CIO launched a campaign to discredit the *Post*. The *Post* was accused of spreading five "lies" that had been identified by the U.S. Office of Facts and Figures as typical of the "Hitler Lie Machine." The *Post* had discouraged the sale of war bonds on the theory that the money would eventually go into the pockets of "union racketeers," urged that the U.S. Army be recalled from overseas and posited that the United States should leave "Hitler's slaves to their fate." The paper attacked Roosevelt, the Supreme Court, the NLRB and the War Labor Board, according to the IUMSWA article. The *Post* also attempted to create "racial disunity by provoking prejudice against the yard's 6,000 negro workers" and even suggested that Russia should sue for a separate peace with Hitler. These allegations were transmitted to one Clyde Tolson, assistant to J. Edgar Hoover, "who immediately turned the facts over to the U.S. Attorney General." What use Hoover and the attorney general made of these wild charges is not recorded in the *Shipyard Worker*. By the fall of 1942, things had become heated in the Wilmington area. Banner headlines proclaimed to workers leaving the yard with copies of the union paper: "*Wilmington Post* cited to FBI as subversive; Faces Probe by Government." Little, however was done by the FBI in the matter, and no further record of the incident appears in the *Shipyard Worker*.[100]

As the hearing in Wilmington progressed, the union called a number of shipyard workers to testify. William R. Dosher Jr., son of the Wilmington postmaster, "created a sensation" when he testified that the North Carolina Shipbuilding Company personnel director "had ask him to act as a labor spy." North Carolina Shipbuilding Company official Bruce Cameron had also urged Dosher to do "all he could to keep the union out of the shipyard." Under examination Dosher stated that it was Robert E. Burnett who had asked him to attend IUMSWA meetings and to report back to the company the members present. Oliver J. Carroll stated also on the stand that he was told by quarterman William J. Kinkaid that if Burnett learned that Carroll was a IUMSWA member he would be fired so "fast his head would spin." Burnett denied any such involvement on the part of the company both at the hearing and in an interview with the writer.[101]

At the hearing, William A. Wright also told of being intimidated by the North Carolina Shipbuilding Company officials. Wright stated that his instructor at the welding school introduced him to a "Mr. Ellis," who proceeded to lecture him for twenty minutes on the virtues of the Cape Fear Union and the shortcomings of the CIO. Two other workers, Porter L. Fuller and Charles R. Frazier, stated that prior membership in a CIO textile union made them undesirable at the North Carolina Shipbuilding Company yard. An unnamed personnel official told Fuller and Frazier that "we don't want your kind down here."[102]

Considerable testimony related to the Cape Fear Union was taken at the hearing. Numerous irregularities were uncovered at the trial in the union's financial dealings. C.W. Page, the union's secretary, stated the *Wilmington Post* agreed to publish a newspaper for the union at no cost. The company union paper contained a large ad placed by one "Macmillan and Cameron." Page stated, "Mr. Cameron of the firm is the same Cameron who is a director of the North Carolina Shipbuilding Company." Page also related that while he handled all the funds of the union, he could not recall when he made the first deposit to the union's account in the bank. Page was similarly unable to furnish any records, ledgers or account books for the union. Numerous irregularities in financial dealings such as this came out in the various NLRB hearings whenever Page was called to testify. The effect of Page's testimony left little doubt in the minds of the NLRB examiners that the Cape Fear union was in fact supported and organized by the North Carolina Shipbuilding Company.[103]

Some 2,381 pages of testimony were taken at the first Wilmington trial, which lasted from October 15 until November 3. The trial was "a topic of hot discussion throughout the community, since practically every home has a member of the family or relative working in the yard." The CIO union was confident of victory over the Cape Fear Union. On the final day of the hearing, P.F. Halsey, general manager of the North Carolina Shipbuilding Company, announced that two employees (Mr. Cooper, an instructor in the welding school, and the aforementioned Ellis) were disciplined for their attempts at intimidating a government witness. The two, according to Halsey, were "suspended for a full week without pay" because of "action highly improper and in disobedience of positive company instructions."[104]

Joseph L. Hecktoen, the NLRB examiner, found that the Newport News and North Carolina Shipbuilding companies were guilty of violating the Wagner Act. Hecktoen recommended that North Carolina Shipbuilding Company withdraw any recognition it had granted the Cape Fear Union and that the six men fired for union activity be rehired. The seventh man, Blake, had joined the marines, so he could not be rehired, but he was awarded back pay along with the others. Fuller and Frazier, former CIO members, were ordered hired by the company under the intermediate report. The company was to post notice of the report and to cease any unfair or discriminatory practice against the IUMSWA.[105]

The IUMSWA, soon after the issuance of the intermediate report by the trial examiner, filed for an early recognition election with the NLRB. The North Carolina Shipbuilding Company countered by filing requests for extensions to determine the size and composition of the bargaining unit. At a hearing held in Wilmington on May 27 and 29, the IUMSWA presented signature cards in sufficient number to "assure a collective bargaining agency election." After numerous alleged harassments and delaying tactics, the election was finally held on September 3, 1942.[106]

In a letter written to the NLRB on July 28, 1943, Lyman Covert, district director of the IUMSWA, included two remarks that were made by North Carolina Shipbuilding Company agents that had given aid to anti-union forces. Covert cited in the letter that Harriss Newman, counsel for North Carolina Shipbuilding Company, replied to a question from NLRB field examiner Irving Hebling, claiming, "We want to wait five or six months to give the new organizations [United Shipbuilders of America—the old Cape Fear Union] an opportunity to take over membership of the Cape Fear Shipbuilders Association, Inc." P.F. Halsey, general manager of the yard, had similarly stated to Hebling, "We can't agree to a consent election. We believe that the whole thing should be delayed two years, or until after the war is over." Covert concluded his plea to the NLRB by stating,

> *Why must board procedure always work to the advantage of those openly opposed to the National Labor Relations Act?...All other parties are getting what they ask for except the organization that has been here more than a year doing everything it could to bring the benefits of a legitimate union and effective collective bargaining to a large group of shipyard workers in the deep South.*[107]

The direction of the election was decided by the NLRB on July 12, 1943, in case R-5455. Three unions had petitioned the NLRB: IUMSWA, the metal trades department of the AFL and the United Shipbuilders of America, Inc. (abbreviated as USA and listed as "an unaffiliated labor organization"). The board's ruling defined the appropriate bargaining unit, outlined the company and unions involved and found that sections 9(c) and 2(b) and 7 of the Wagner Act could be applied to the Wilmington case. Under 9(c), the board ordered that "an election by secret ballot among the employees...shall be conducted as early as possible...to determine whether they desire to be represented by the CIO... AFL or by United Shipbuilders of America, Inc. for the purpose of collective bargaining or by none." The employees of the yard were to be given the choice of the three unions or no union at all. The majority chose the latter in an election.[108]

The appropriate bargaining unit for purposes of the election was defined by the NLRB to exclude "all employees of the administrative, comptroller, auditing and bookkeeping, tabulating, treasurer's, bond, production, safety, welfare, deferment, personnel, timekeeping and job training departments." Similarly, "all material and tool checkers, storekeepers, draftsmen, chemists, clerks and stenographers and all employees of the clinic or medical department except janitors" were to be excluded from participation in the election. All militarized (i.e., coast guard reserve) and plant-protection employees of the yard were also excluded from the unit. Student workers at the training school, as well as members of the transportation department, were to be included in the bargaining unit. The board stated its position:

> *We find that all production and maintenance employees of the Company at its Wilmington, North Carolina Shipyards, including drivers in the transportation department, students and apprentices, but excluding supervisors of the rank of leadingman and above, blue print, timekeeping, job training, piece-work counting, time-study and plant protection employees, progressmen, draftsmen, chemists, material and tool checkers, storekeepers, medical department employees except janitors, and all other clerical and technical employees with authority to hire, promote, discharge, discipline or otherwise effect changes in the status of employees, or effectively recommend such action, constitute a unit appropriate for the purposes of collective bargaining within the meaning of Section 9(b) of the Act.*[109]

This decision effectively resolved the question of exclusions, which was a hotly contested issue amid the company, the CIO, the AFL and the USA. In general, the CIO sought to exclude all students and employees not in actual ship production, erection and maintenance. The AFL wanted to include certain classes of white collar foremen and "other intermediate grades of supervisory employees" and miscellaneous and sundry people such as "the supervisor in the War Bond department and the chief, lieutenant, sergeant and assistant chief in the plant protection department." The USA unit was similar to the AFL bargaining unit but also included orderlies, nurses, secretaries and cost accountants, but excluded all supervisory personnel above the rank of leadingman. Obviously, the unions involved wanted to include favorable units and exclude those groups thought to favor rival unions. The company appeared on the surface at least to have taken a neutral stance, requiring only that supervisory personnel be exempted. However, with the company's involvement in the USA their exclusions became of some interest. The USA wanted to include secretaries, nurses and accountants—groups that would tend to favor a company decision. The NLRB, however, ruled that members of the medical, "auditing, comptroller, bookkeeping and tabulation and clerical" departments be excluded from the bargaining unit. The company's attempt at padding the rolls, then, failed.[110]

William M. Aicher, NLRB regional director, stated in his report of the results of the September 3 election, that of the 14,800 eligible workers in the plant, some 11,210 voted in the election. The IUMSWA received 4,037 votes, the AFL 457 votes, and the USA ran a poor third with 88 votes. "No union" garnered 6,628 votes. Since the CIO did not receive a majority of the votes cast, the attorneys for the IUMSWA filed an objection to the conduct of the election.[111]

H.M. Goldstein, speaking for the IUMSWA, in his petition to the NLRB alleged that employees of North Carolina Shipbuilding Company "were subjected to physical violence and threats of violence by other employees of the Company who had…been given free rein by the company…on behalf of the Cape Fear and United Shipbuilders." He had also stated that the mayor of Wilmington, "one Cameron," had "promised that every person participating in activities to keep the

CIO out of the yard…would be well taken care of." Members of a task force—organized at North Carolina Shipbuilding Company to keep the CIO out—were alleged to have been at a meeting held in the office of an attorney Stevens "in the Murchison Building, Wilmington on the morning of either Friday, August 27th or Saturday, August 28th." Company "goons" were to be permitted "ingress and egress thereto and therefrom [the yard] as they might desire and…if they ran into any trouble they were to communicate with the said Stevens and with one Walker, the Sheriff of New Hanover County." The petition by Goldstein went on to state that "pursuant to the foregoing plot…the aforesaid attendants…did…during the conduct of the said election…threaten and intimidate the employees desiring to vote with dire consequences if they did not vote against the petitioners and did distribute literature urging the employees to vote against the CIO." The petition further stated, "Numerous supervisors of the company congregated throughout the time of the balloting and urged the employees to vote against the petitioner." Goldstein claimed that a group of supervisory employees led by one "old man Henry" (Badge #69-022) did "threaten physical violence to the regional director of the fifth region [William M. Aicher of the NLRB] and other board agents." All this of course, was in direct violation of Wagner Act election safeguards.[112]

Roger Williams, in a long letter to the NLRB on December 2, 1943, responded to the CIO contention of election law violations. Williams felt that setting aside the election would "seriously disrupt the major war effort which is our paramount concern." Williams also stated that the North Carolina Shipbuilding Company had followed a policy of "strict neutrality" in the election. The rest of the letter continued to respond to the charge outlined by Goldstein in the IUMSWA petition of September 13, 1943. On November 10, 1943, the NLRB trial examiner, Mr. Aicher, issued a report that affirmed the petition of the IUMSWA. Aicher recommended "that the results of the election…be set aside [and that] serious consideration be given to the prosecution of Hendricks under Section 12 of the [Wagner] Act." Hendricks ("old man Henry"), it is recalled, was charged with attacking the NLRB election conductors. Williams pointed out that while Aicher referred to improper action by the company "on several occasions," in point of fact there was only the single occurrence on the morning of September 4. The president of the yard related that as soon as the incident Goldstein referred to occurred, he took steps to stop such activities:

> *It appears that the occurrence on which the IUMSWA objection and Mr. Aicher's recommendation are based took place shortly before 4:00 A.M., Mr. Aicher got in touch with Mr. R.L. Burnett, Employment Manager; that Mr. Burnett returned with Mr. Aicher to Polling Place No. 2; that a short discussion ensued during which Mr. Burnett told Hendricks that the Board representatives were conducting the election and the Company had nothing to do with it; that he told Hendricks to leave the vicinity of the polling place and not to comeback; and that so far as the Company is able to determine, Hendricks complied with these directions.*[113]

According to North Carolina Shipbuilding Company investigations, the threatened violence by "old man Henry" amounted to at most a verbal dressing down. Williams went on to argue that only two or three hundred people were lined up at the polling place when the incident occurred. The election had already been going on for twenty-two hours and had four more to run. The company estimated that not more than 300 votes were cast that morning at Polling Place No. 2. Since a shift of 1,296 votes would have been needed for the IUMSWA to win, the company reasoned that this would not have occurred as a result of any change in conditions at Polling Place No. 2.

North Carolina Shipbuilding Company further argued that the NLRB election of September 3 and 4 should not have been set aside because of alleged company interference. The company contended that the incident also had not been given wide publicity by the local press. (IUMSWA officials would no doubt agree with that!) Williams pointed out that "the company was commended and congratulated by representatives of the Board after completion of the election and before the counting of the ballots." The letter commended the NLRB employee Aicher for his interest in being on hand and supervision of the election at 4:00 a.m. The company also felt that while Aicher had a right to be resentful of North Carolina Shipbuilding Company personnel who abused him, he did not have the right to set aside the election based on that one fact alone. North Carolina Shipbuilding Company hoped that with the aid of "time and peace gaining it a proper perspective," the NLRB in Washington would let the results of the election stand. Williams concluded his memorial by stating that

> *as you and the other members of the Board must realize the Company and its management deplore the action of Hendricks far more than is possible in the case of any of the individuals directly concerned. That action apparently threatens to cancel the results of our most earnest effort and to bring upon this plant at its most critical period of conversion from liberty ship to a much more difficult type of vessel all of the confusion, diversion of effort, excitement of animosities and possibility of physical violence which will be the inevitable incidence of another election. The company will do anything within its power to comply with any reasonable request which the Board or Mr. Aicher may make to redress the personal affront which he has suffered from one of the company's employees. This, however, should not require setting aside an election in which over 11,000 men participated and seriously disrupting the major war effort which is our paramount concern.*[114]

The *Shipyard Worker*, on the other hand, reported that Hendricks engaged in "a violent altercation" with Aicher. Aicher was quoted as saying that "Hendricks used language of such an incendiary nature as to constitute actual incitement to mob violence. During the several minutes' duration of this incident, direct threats of physical violence were made against the director" of the election. The paper referred later to the fact that Aicher had, as the headline put it, "Hit Company Goons." It was alleged that "company goons and thugs had not only intimidated the workers against the IUMSWA during the poll, but had also openly threatened the representative of the NLRB."[115]

In the midst of the IUMSWA attempts at having the election set aside, an event occurred that gave the union cause for hope. In December 1943, North Carolina Shipbuilding Company agreed to reinstate with back pay nine workers of the Wilmington yard who the IUMSWA alleged had been fired because of union activity. Several union members received settlements ranging from $1,900 to $3,000. The next issue of the *Shipyard Worker* featured on the front page the North Carolina Shipbuilding Company checks to brothers Mack Reynolds, Solomon Hazel and James Scott. The article went on to proclaim that "reinstated union members stand proudly in N.C. Yard." The workers were reinstated in their former jobs and received back pay for time lost when they were prevented from working in the yard. Of the nine reinstated, one had entered the marines, as previously mentioned, and another, Harry White, was employed as an inspector for the Maritime Commission. The remaining seven testified to their loyalty to the union and chronicled how the had "kept faith in unions" over the long months. All were confident of union victory and stopped in frequently at the union hall to inquire "What's cooking?" during their long period without work.[116]

Most of the workers receiving reinstated pay invested their windfall in U.S. savings bonds. The *Shipyard Worker* of December 31, 1945, showed the smiling faces of Mack Reynolds and William Parker, as they clutched $2,400 worth of war bonds. One of the fortunate related that "Uncle Sam has stuck by me and now I'm sticking by him. I am buying War Bonds with mine." Another soul went out and purchased the farm he had been "a-hankering for." This ardent pro-unionist stated how long he had wanted a farm and had come near getting one before, if it had not been for "Herbert Hoover's administration. I have had my eye on a little spot of land out here for some time. Now I have enough for a down payment and the first bag of potatoes I put down will have a CIO label on them."[117]

IUMSWA national organizer Bruce Davis stated that "one can fully appreciate the happy faces of all these brothers, it was plenty tough at home during the long drawn out fight. And now to see their happiness at the prospect of obtaining the homes they desire, of buying more War Bonds, of getting their kids some clothes for Christmas, gives one a very warm feeling inside." The end of 1943 saw the IUMSWA hopes at Wilmington boosted by advances such as these. Hopes were high for a new election and eventual CIO union victory at North Carolina Shipbuilding Company.[118]

Labor relations at the yard became molded by the end of 1943 into a typical pattern of the national labor-management conflict. There were the usual Southern anti-black, anti-union overtones present in addition at Wilmington. The September 1943 NLRB election mirrored the anti-union majority at the Wilmington yard. Roger Williams reported another aspect of yard union activity at the Truman committee hearings in March 1943. In a statement to Senate aide Albert C. Hill on March 9, Williams answered the query as to what he would do to increase American shipyard production by stating he would "freeze present labor organization for the duration." Williams related that "in his plant there is an independent union and CIO is attempting to organize it. The younger supervisors resent the CIO and favor independent organization; as a result the firm has been cited for unfair practices."[119]

The story according to Williams was that the company was caught in a power play between CIO organizers and the Cape Fear Shipbuilders backed by lower rank company supervisors. Williams felt that while the company was not doing anything wrong, the "younger supervisors" in their zeal to keep the CIO out were by their aid to the Cape Fear Union causing the company to be cited by the CIO. The shipyard always praised the work of its employees, and Williams stated that the best workers in the United States came from the country stock of North Carolina. This praise of company workers as the "best" is contrasted at the same time with the allegations of the CIO and statements of company officers regarding the amount of time they spent in company involvement in the independent union. Homer Ferguson stated that 98 percent of his time was spent on "personnel problems." "I don't get to do much work," lamented Ferguson the shipbuilder. The union issue was hotly debated in Wilmington and left many scars. As late as 1975, P.F. Halsey, the vice-president and general manager of North Carolina Shipbuilding Company, was very bitter over the union issue. He stated that "the Communist dominated" union racketeers were responsible for the company's difficulties. In 1943, however, the CIO was optimistic about their chances in the Wilmington yard.[120]

The conflict between the independents, the CIO, the AFL and the company continued until 1944. Two cases were now before the NLRB: a new representation case (5-R-1528) and the continued unfair labor practice case (5-C-1565). The representation case was decided in 1944; the unfair labor practice case dragged on until 1946, long after the yard had closed down. The pattern of union conflict in 1943 was repeated in 1944 and continued until the end of production. The CIO would complain of unfair practices and petition for a new election. The company would respond by petitioning for a delay in the election and issue a denial of the unfair practice. When the yard closed at Wilmington in 1946, the struggle was carried to the Newport News yard where it continues today.[121]

In mid-1943, the AFL had filed a brief with the NLRB for a motion for reconsideration as the bargaining agent at Wilmington. The AFL stated that because certain skills—where the AFL was strong—were excluded by the NLRB from the election, the AFL received a poor showing. It should be recalled that the AFL received only 457 out of 14,800 eligible votes. The AFL felt that piecework counters, timekeepers, material checkers, tool checkers, storekeepers, draftsmen, chemists, clerks, stenographers, leading men and quartermen should all be members of the AFL bargaining unit. These special skills, while not all actual ship construction labor, were composed of members taken from common labor ranks in some cases (i.e. piecework counters, materials checkers) or were members of bargaining units on West Coast and Great Lakes yards. By expanding representation, the AFL hoped to gain a greater voice in labor at the Wilmington yard.[122]

On April 18, 1944, the NLRB regional attorney filed a brief with the assistant general counsel of the NLRB, calling for a hearing to be conducted into the request for representation filed by the IUMSWA. Once again the questions of the rival unions as well as the size of the bargaining unit were raised. In reaching his recommendation, Attorney Earle K. Shawe took note of the prior "R" case decision

(R-5455)—the unfair labor practice case that resulted in the back pay settlement (C-2500)—and the then-pending second unfair labor practice case (5-C-1565). The hearing so directed was held in Wilmington on Thursday, April 27, 1944. At the hearing, D.B. Kelly, a representative of the Wilmington AFL Metal Trades Council, dropped a bombshell when he announced that the AFL "would call on its members to vote for the IUMSWA-CIO." According to the *Shipyard Worker*, both "the company and the company union, with their attorneys were dumbstruck" when Kelly announced that "the American Federation of Labor does not choose to be on the ballot and is thus withdrawing from the hearing." AFL members were urged to vote for the IUMSWA union. CIO men, of course, were jubilant. IUMSWA leaders commended the AFL: "This is the sort of unity that will advance the cause of labor in the State of North Carolina." Apparently, AFL officials and rank-and-file members felt they would much rather see bona fide labor organization, IUMSWA-CIO, represent the workers of the yard than a company union.[123]

On February 25, 1944, the CIO withdrew its objection to the prior election and filed an application for a new election. On March 1, 1944, the NLRB issued a "Decision and Order of Dismissal" rejecting the petition of the IUMSWA. On April 4, the NLRB's fifth regional director, Ross Madden and Attorney Earle Shawe concurred in a letter to Oscar Smith, director of the NLRB field operations, that "it is our recommendation that the petitioning union is entitled to another election at this time in view of the entire background of the case." The regional office went on to state that while the CIO could not win another election in view of their poor representation in the September election (30 percent), "they are asking for it and it is our feeling that they are entitled to it." Madden pointed out that North Carolina Shipbuilding Company took the position that the recent election showed the correct strength of the union and that the company should be "permitted to concentrate all of its efforts toward the building of ships." The CIO responded by stating that "there is an active campaign in progress and cards are coming in [from new members] daily."[124]

In its decision on June 29, 1944, the board replied that the size of the unit should be expanded to include orderlies in the medical department, material men in the operating departments and tool keepers. Messengers, materials checkers, storekeepers, timekeepers and piecework counters were excluded from the unit, as in the R-5455 case. All petitioners desired to include orderlies, material men and tool keepers, while the CIO wanted to exclude the messengers, material checkers, storekeepers, timekeepers and piecework counters. The company and the USA wanted to expand the unit to encompass all those listed above. The board sided with the CIO and directed that an election by secret ballot be held within thirty days pursuant to section 9(c) of the Wagner Act.[125]

Concurrently, the Liberty shipbuilding program was coming to an end, and the conversion to the Victory C-2 program was beginning. Anticipating fewer contracts, the company began discharging employees. The CIO charged that the company was firing only union members. The union stressed the apparent contradiction in the fact that North Carolina Shipbuilding Company was firing workers, while at the same time the War Manpower Commission was seeking to solve a supposed labor shortage in the Wilmington area. Wilmington had been placed in the number-one labor shortage category by the WMC. The number one category was the highest and most critical category the commission could assign for labor shortages. The IUMSWA also claimed that North Carolina Shipbuilding Company had refused to rehire those it knew to be union members. The union claimed that the company had in its records "some indication of whether the company's former workers were members of the IUMSWA." The union filed a new unfair labor practices charge with the NLRB, the WMC and the Maritime Commission. A delegation of laid-off workers met with North Carolina Governor J. Melville Broughton at Raleigh and brought the unfair labor charges before him. Specifically, the union officials and workers wanted to know if the layoffs were justified at that time, if it was able to employ a full manpower commission worker utilization survey and if it could halt to recruiting of more workers by the U.S. Employment Service (USES) at the same time layoffs were in progress. Some departments in the yard had to go to nine- and ten-hour shifts to overcome the lack of workers, union organizers pointed out. The governor stated that he would personally institute an investigation into the layoffs at the yard. Regional directors of the War Manpower Commission and USES quickly promised that the requests would be honored. As a result of this unfavorable publicity, North Carolina Shipbuilding Company suddenly put an end to mass layoffs.[126]

At this point in July 1944, the NLRB had ordered a new election to be held within thirty days at the North Carolina Shipbuilding Company. However, before an election would be held, the IUMSWA wanted to make certain that the unfair labor practices against its members by the company were brought to an end. An election would be pointless if workers could be secretly coerced by members of company management as it was alleged in the past.[127]

On July 20, 1944, the NLRB issued an amended order that indefinitely postponed the election pending at the North Carolina Shipbuilding Company. The board had been advised by its regional director that an election "could not appropriately be held at this time." Ross Madden stated later that the board issued "an order postponing indefinitely the holding of the election because of the pending of unfair labor practice" case. In short, the NLRB upheld the union request for a delay to prevent the coercion of workers in a yard where workers had been intimidated in the past by the company. The company had wanted the election postponed because of the "war effort." The indefinite delay proved permanent. The election order against the company was finally withdrawn after the plant had shut down in late 1946.[128]

Postponement of the second representation election set the stage for the final and largest scene in the IUMSWA drama at Wilmington. The union now concentrated its efforts in the large unfair labor practices case. If the IUMSWA could obtain an unfair practice ruling, this would have major impact on CIO representation at both Wilmington and Newport News. The opening of these two yards to the CIO would in turn have a major effect on labor representation in the Southern yards. Much was at stake both for the CIO and Newport News Shipbuilding. The resulting trial proved the enormity of the issue.

The unfair labor practice hearing opened in Wilmington at the federal courthouse on January 8, 1945, and became one of the longest in the history of the NLRB. The hearings ended on July 18, after ninety-six days of testimony. The record of the trial preserved in the Federal National Records Center, Suitland, Maryland, is truly monumental in scope. A total of 668 witnesses testified at the hearing. On direct initial examination, the CIO produced 145 witnesses while the North Carolina Shipbuilding Company called 421. The IUMSWA called 77 witnesses back to the stand for rebuttal.[129]

The first witness called for the company was P.F. Halsey, vice-president and general manager of North Carolina Shipbuilding Company. Halsey's initial testimony consisted mainly of technical information on yard operations. As such, it is a valuable source of information regarding Liberty ship construction. The second witness called on behalf of the company was the personnel manager of the yard, J. Weaver Kirkpatrick. Kirkpatrick explained the standard personnel practices in force at the yard. Attempts at proving irregularities such as special marks on CIO member employment records and other efforts demonstrating open anti-union activity on behalf of the company met with failure during Kirkpatrick's testimony.[130]

The first witness called in behalf of the union was a former quarterman in the erector's division, Archie T. Pruitt. Pruitt testified that it was his job to look out for CIO activity in the yard and to turn in any CIO members he could find for discharge by the company. Pruitt stated that he was instructed "to keep the CIO the hell out of the yard." If he was successful in this venture, "he would be taken care of by the company." Pruitt testified that he was told that "if the CIO gets into the yard, the Company would cease operation…close it down and send them all back to Newport News." In the specific instance of the discharge of one of the parties to the CIO suit, Pruitt related that he "asked him why and he said they discharged him for being a CIO man. He said they got the goods on him and they let him go." Pruitt was subjected to cross-examination by the company, but lawyers were unable to shake his testimony after three days on the stand. Pruitt admitted, however, that he was discharged because "he told a fellow supervisor that he hoped the CIO would win the NLRB election." Pruitt's testimony proved rather damaging to the company's case.[131]

The next witness was a minister, James H. Hale. Hale stated that he was discharged for making the remark that "any man had the right to belong to an organization of his own choosing" and the Cape Fear Union "could do the working man no good." The following witness, John J. Pruden, also a quarterman in the erector's department, testified that when his son's CIO card fell out of his pocket at the yard, he was promptly fired by the company. Other workers at the yard, such as Clarence Hare and John W. Curtis, testified under oath that they were to turn in to the personnel office the name of any CIO member they discovered. Curtis related that when he protested the discharge of CIO members, he was promptly fired. In all these cases, the supervisors named P.F. Halsey as the "top man in the anti-IUMSWA espionage system set up in the North Carolina yard."[132]

The CIO continued to parade witness after witness who all testified to the anti-union activities of the yard. George Crooms and Leroy Hooks reported on

George Crooms, with yellow Model A Ford and "Little John L. Lewis" (rattlesnake) in the cage. The caption on the cage reads, "Never let it be said that this Duck is Dead." The cage (Mr. Bracy's "Rabbit Box") was built by Harry Livingston on company time and out of NCSB materials according to testimony given at the NLRB hearing. Croom told workers leaving the yard over a loudspeaker "Tell the Working Class People not to get to close…that he would strike!"

the stand that they joined the CIO for the purpose of gaining information on the names of other CIO members, names they then turned over to Halsey. Hooks "succumbed to tears" on the stand while "trying to conceal his perfidy" according to CIO accounts. Hooks stated first that he was drunk when he signed the CIO card and didn't know what he was doing. However, Hooks next testified to the court that he didn't drink. At this point Hooks suffered another lapse of memory, which frequently characterized his testimony. Hooks was labeled "Special Organizer for the company union" and a "professional stooge" by the CIO.[133]

"Another witness to the espionage system," Herbert T. Schibben, alleged that at the hearing Robert Burnett, employment manager at North Carolina Shipbuilding Company, asked him, "What are you doing here?" Schibben replied, "I am here to testify for the union and the government." Burnett was reported to have stated in reply, "Why don't you go back home? You know your home is here and your people will feel hard against you if you testify against them." Schibben revealed this intimidation of a witness during the trial on the stand under oath.[134]

During the fifth week of the trial, union witnesses alleged that the draft was used as a weapon against union members and that defective vessels were delivered to the Maritime Commission in an attempt at hiding the delays caused by the loss of production due to the firing of union members. Richard Shew, organizer for the Cape Fear Union, testified that he was told by Bruce Cameron to get rid of "all CIO men even if it meant getting them put in the draft." Shew also stated that even though he was employed as a machinist in the yard, his real job 50 percent of the time was to organize the Cape Fear Company Union. He stated that he reported his union activities to Bruce Cameron, former mayor of Wilmington and a director of the North Carolina Shipbuilding Company. Shew stated also that Richard Burnett instructed him not to give draft deferments to CIO members.[135]

Shew also testified as to the poor condition of vessels leaving the Wilmington yard:

> *I was working on the steering, on the steering engine, and our duties were to clean up the engine and adjust the bearings and get the ship, the engine, in shape, and more or less break it in. But it seemed that it was taking quite a bit of time on these particular jobs, and on numerous occasions the bearings, even when the engine would be running properly, would be taken out and filed, or they would take the shims out, and the next thing we knew about it, why, it would be running hot, and then we would have to work way into the night to get overtime, and we worked on practically every engine, we would work, seven, eight, ten hours overtime, six hours overtime, five hours overtime.*
>
> *And we fellows got to talking among ourselves that it was more or less being drug out to create overtime employment by our supervisor. And I knew that sooner or later there would be—they were going to mess up one of the engines so bad they couldn't stop it, and it finally happened at Hull 75, the Steamship Matt Ransom.*
>
> *We went to work on this particular ship after three o'clock, about three o'clock we started breaking it in. We worked until about eleven o'clock that night, and we thought the engine was all right—wasn't perfect, but enough to get it by the next morning for the Maritime test.*
>
> *Before we had the Maritime test about twelve o'clock this Mr. Staples, Harry Staples, called us all down and wanted to run the engine some. I don't know what transpired in the engine room, as I was up in the wheel house. But we got—we were up there pulling it over by the wheel from right rudder to left rudder, and finally we got a call over the telephone to stop everything and come down to the engine room.*
>
> *The engine had froze up. I was told by one of the boys Louis Barnes, in the steering gear room, that Staples had taken out the shims under it, tightened down the bearings—had Odum tighten the bearings until it froze up hard and fast.*
>
> *We all got in together to take—the Maritime test was coming off at twelve o'clock, I think it was that day, and Staples said he had to have it ready for this Maritime test, and he was going to get it by some way.*

> *We took off, saw the condition, saw the brass ground into the shaft. We asked—Staples says, "We have to fix it." So we cleaned it up the best we could, put it back on, and Odum left the caps loose.*
>
> *We got by the Maritime test by the skin of our teeth. The caps were jumping up and down during the test. Staples said, "If I can get it by this Maritime test, I will fix it this morning."*
>
> *The next, I believe, or the day after, I believe the ship lay there two days before she sailed, and I thought any minute we would have to take the shaft out. I was on this other ship alongside of 65 when Staples came over...I said, "My God, they are not going to let that ship go out in that condition?" He said, "Hell, yes." I said, "My God." He said, "They won't go far with that. I feel sorry for those bastards, not knowing what they have under them." I said, "What did Mr. Baysden say?" He said, "Mr. Baysden said the Maritime inspector had accepted it. It was the Maritime Commission's baby, and let them handle it."*
>
> *I didn't—when I could get away from Staples I went to the general office and called on the telephone and got Naval Intelligence and had the ship stopped at South Port. Now I have been informed that they had to put in a new shaft and new bearings at South Port before the ship could go out of the harbor.*[136]

Shew stated that he had been threatened with a loss of his job if he told anyone about the defect. Shew became increasingly dissatisfied with the yard, but remained on the job because Cameron told him he was doing an excellent job of "keeping the CIO out" of the yard. Shew also reported to Halsey and Cameron that various "bosses" had removed company property for their private use. Specifically, Oliver C. Staples had used 150 feet of 12-inch steel pipe for a drainpipe in his private residence, and "copper frying pans" and "stew pots for stewing chickens" were made out of 1/8-inch sheet copper owned by the company. Needless to say, steel pipe and 1/8-inch copper sheets were in short supply during the war. Burnett, however, related that this was a common practice in the yard. He displayed an iron grate made in the yard for his fireplace given to him as a gift by yard employees. Fashioning gifts out of surplus materials was a rather common occurrence at Maritime Commission yards. For his pains as an undercover agent, Shew was transferred to the north yard, where he erected operating rods on a high scaffold. He was told that this new position was temporary "until the fellow that had done the work before could recover from a fall he had taken the week before when the scaffold fell with him." Shew did not remain on the scaffold long after that and soon quit his job.[137]

Similar cases of high hazard work assigned to those who "fell out" with the company were reported at the hearing. Wallace Burdette, a former painter at North Carolina Shipbuilding Company, told of what became of him when he joined the CIO and the company found out about it. Burdette testified that he was transferred from the north yard to paint inside a tank "possibly twelve or eighteen inches in diameter that you had to crawl in and out and through to get up in them. And some of them I would say was maybe five or six feet in length, and two or three feet in width. But they had—maybe thirty or forty different compartments in one tank."

Burdette continued his testimony:

Q. Would you take a light in there with you to see by?
A. Yes sir; we had a light.
Q. In what position would you apply the paint?
A. In a crouch position, sitting down or laying down. Some places it was pretty tough; others you could probably sit down and throw your neck down and lean over on your elbow and do the work.
Q. Were you using a brush, or a spray gun?
A. In the inner bottoms we were using a brush.
Q. Did you spend all your time on a shift on the inner bottoms or did you come out?
A. We didn't spend all our time in the inner bottoms.
Q. Explain that?
A. We never had no instructions to come out. When we come out we come out on our own. In fact I had been told several times not to be caught out.
Q. What did you do for air?
A. Well, whenever I got to where I felt I needed it, I come out.
Q. How often did you come out?
A. I would say every hour to hour and a half.[138]

When Burdette asked why he was placed in such an uncomfortable work, he was told that it was because he "was a CIO member." Burdette and other CIO men soon became ill in the confined spaces and reported their health problems to P.F. Halsey:

*Well, I told Mr. Halsey the conditions and the way we had been treated, and that we would like for him to make an investigation. And he said it was the first he had ever heard of any mistreatment in Mr. Neill's department. I told him, "Well," I said—I told him all about the *iggers being pulled out of the tanks and us being put down in there and to use that we knew it was because we were union men, or thought to be union men, and that we thought it was our duty to go up and ask him to make an investigation, that it was nothing but because we were associated with the union, or they thought we was. And Mr. Halsey…seems as if he got angry…Or at least Mr. Halsey made an attempt to rise from his chair, and said "This yard is a no union yard, and it will stay that way." And then he sat back down and took it a little easier.*[139]

On February 7–9, a key union witness, Manuel Marquess, implicated the company in several unfair labor practices. Marquess alleged that the employment records of CIO members were marked with a red pencil and "placed in a separate drawer." When it came time for layoffs, Marquess alleged that this system enabled the company to determine quickly who the CIO men were. Marquess also implicated P.F. Halsey in the company "stooge" spy system. Marquess claimed that he was the target of numerous attempts at coercion while he was waiting in Wilmington to testify at the trial. Marquess stated that he was offered numerous opportunities to leave town by "company goons" but that he stayed in spite of the threats. McLendon and Burnett were also accused of coercing a witness at the trial by Marsden Ward. While the two denied the coercion, Ward maintained in court that "You know you did this thing," as he pointed a finger toward McLendon.[140]

As the trial continued, CIO men testified that the "racial issue" was used to get men to join the USA. James Bass stated that a USA organizer told him, "I want you to join the USA. If the CIO comes in, you will have a colored boss, and white people will be forced to work with colored people." Bass was terminated shortly after he refused to join the USA. Assistant Foreman Pulley called Bass "nothing but a CIO lover" just prior to his discharge. The USA was not integrated as the CIO was, but had a separate "colored division" for blacks.[141]

Workers continued to come forth and testify as to beatings and intimidation of CIO members. Fred Smith testified that during the NLRB election, while he was a poll-watcher for the CIO, he was sent out of the yard by the company to get a pack of cigarettes. Outside the gate he was met by "prize fighter Red Nichols and Bill Williams," who proceeded to "knock out two or three of his teeth." Hayner Lennon and other CIO men in the transportation department testified that they had been put to work lifting rails that had been formerly lifted by cranes. Lennon stated that "he had an operation and that the heavy lifting further injured him, causing him to terminate. The other CIO men were forced to leave also, because of the extremely hard work."[142]

Perhaps the most amazing testimony is that of Harry Livingston. Livingston stated that he was pressured into turning in the names of CIO members by his supervisor. Livingston's testimony speaks of building a cage on company time that later turned up on George Crooms's yellow Model T parked at the yard gate with anti-union propaganda on it.

> *Me and a fellow by the name of Blake was a working together and Mr. Bracy came over and got Mr. Blake and told him he had another job for him, and put him to work, and told me to continue what I was doing, and Mr. Blake couldn't complete the job by knocking off time, and Mr. Bracy came over and got me and I went over and saw Mr. Blake building some kind of cage concern and I asked him what it was and he turned it off and laughed and said, "Oh, a rabbit box," and I had never seen any cages like that built in the yard or shop before, and it kind of looked suspicious to me…and while we was working on it there was various different people come in and looked at it. While we was working on the cage we needed some material, he had gotten some wire and boards there, got his wire from the sheet metal shed, and we had put it all together but the top on it and we needed some hinges and a hasp and some screws so Mr. Bracy writes out me a written order for a hasp and a set of hinges and I got the screws from out of the material room in the ship and I went over to the store room and while I was going over there I read the order he had gave me, and he had it charged to my number, and the account number was charged "temporary hand rate," is what the material and hinges was charged to, and I got the material from the store room and went back and put it on. I helped Mr. Blake and me and him together put it on, and we worked five minutes after the whistle blowed to get the hinges and hasp*

> *on, and all that was lacking to it was the painting, and we left it on the work bench that afternoon and when I came back for work the next morning I never seen nothing of it.*
> *Q. Did you work on this cage on company time?*
> *A. Yes, sir.*
> *Q. Now, after you were terminated from the yard did you ever see that cage.*
> *A. I saw it on the front of Mr. Crooms' car out in front of the ship yard there…I went to take a look at it myself being as I had helped to build the cage, and all, and I was sort of suspicious, and I drove down a going to work off the dry dock, I drove down to take a look for myself, to see if it was the cage I helped work on, and I drove by, and saw the cage, and I saw a rattlesnake in it, and I saw the CIO button in the bottom, with the rattlesnake, and I heard Crooms say, "Tell the working class people not to get close, that was a little John L. Lewis, that he would strike."*
> *Q. Now, this statement was made by Crooms, was it over a loud speaker?*
> *A. That's right.*[143]

The CIO arguments in the hearings concluded on March 15 when Seaborn Little repeated the usual charges of espionage, intimidation and reporting. Little worked in the splicing ship, the area where the USA office was located. Little testified that the constitution and other records of the USA were kept in the splicing ship in a "little black book." These records pertained to the union position of the men in each unit. Little also testified that Robert Burnett, employment manager, had attended an organizational meeting of the USA in the splicing shop. When USA organizers expressed concern as to what to do at the NLRB trial, Burnett told them, "There will be nothing to the hearing. You have never signed up USA members here, have you? You have never held any meetings here, have you? If you take have to take the stand tell them that you were here discussing a play called Step Lively."[144]

The hearings were recessed from March 15 until April 30 to enable company attorneys to prepare a defense to the long list of CIO allegations. The company witnesses reiterated that no USA union members "were signed up in the yard, that all were signed up outside the yard after working hours." In all the company called some 421 workers, both supervisory and ordinary, to refute the testimony of the IUMSWA witnesses.[145]

The testimony of the North Carolina Shipbuilding Company witnesses supported the claims stated in a brief filed with the NLRB by P.F. Halsey on November 6, 1944. The brief replied directly to certain points raised by the CIO and refuted the testimony of most of the union witnesses. The witnesses denied that the company "discharged or fired or refused to hire employees or prospective employees when their services were needed by it, except in instances in which such discharge, transfers or refusals to hire were for good cause in efficient operation of its business." In short, the company witnesses insisted that there were legitimate reasons, medical or otherwise, why workers were fired. The CIO, of course, contended that North Carolina Shipbuilding Company work had destroyed their health, and then fired these men, because of their CIO activity.[146]

On September 30, 1946, counsel for North Carolina Shipbuilding Company filed a motion for extension of time in order to prepare its answer to the intermediate report and a request for an oral argument before the NLRB. Counsel cited the unusual length of the case and the "novelty of some of the questions involved" as reasons for the delay and for oral argument.[147]

However, on November 8, 1946, slightly over a year after the trial ended, counsel for the company, the CIO, the USA, and the NLRB regional attorney agreed to a settlement stipulation. By this time North Carolina Shipbuilding Company no longer engaged in the production of vessels and was "in process of liquidation and winding up its affairs." North Carolina Shipbuilding Company agreed to the settlement without regard to admitting to any of the allegations contained in the complaint or without admitting that it had committed any unfair labor practices. The company promised to refrain from interfering with the formation of the USA and from contributing to the support of the same. It further pledged to refrain from discouraging membership in the CIO, "discriminating as to hire" because of testimony before the NLRB. North Carolina Shipbuilding Company was to disassociate itself completely from the USA as the representative of any of its employees and place all fifty-one employees named in "Appendix A" on a preferential hiring list. The company further subscribed to the back pay provision of the intermediate report to the tune of $65,000 for the fifty-one named employees. North Carolina Shipbuilding Company was also required to post in "conspicuous places" in the yard copies of a notice outlining the settlement stipulation. Finally, the company was to notify the NLRB the moment it resumed operations at the Wilmington plant. The CIO agreed that the back pay settlement would be sufficient for "satisfaction of all obligations…for any loss of pay which any of the individuals involved…may have suffered by reason of their lay-offs."[148]

Long before the settlement, workers who had testified on behalf of the CIO had given up hope of a favorable outcome. One of the key union witnesses, Archie Pruitt, wrote to NLRB pleading for relief. Pruitt stated, "What I would like to know is when I am going to get any definite concrete results from my complaint if any and if it will be when I am living or after I am dead and have been buried." He continued, "In my estimation…the NLRB has not achieved the purpose for which it was intended…which was the quick and efficient expedition of labor cases pertaining to the Wagner Act…The long drawn out litigation of manufactured presentments and defenses…are an attorney's delight and relishment and are too often a boon to these corporations." Clearly, the patience of workers had long been exhausted by the NLRB trial and legal wrangling that followed. In his reply to Pruitt, NLRB Attorney Avrutis argued that the purpose of the Wagner Act was not to relieve individuals such as Pruitt but to provide a base from which workers could be assured of the rightful place they deserved in the marketplace. Avrutis wrote in his reply of September 17, 1946:

> *I can understand your wish for an early disposition of this matter. However, I do not believe that early closing the shipyards will affect your interest or those of any other employee involved.*

Under the statutory procedure, individual discharges are not considered separately, as you would like to have done in your own instance. It is not the claim of any individual employee but an alleged offense against the public interest, and the rights of employees generally, which is litigated in a Board hearing. Consideration is given to unfair labor practices purely for the sake of protecting that interest, and the rights of employees are safeguarded only as a way to protect the public right. The instances of all employees allegedly discriminated against are considered together. If unfair labor practices have been found, the Board issues an order intended to remedy the entire situation and thereby protect all.

As you will recall, the case took about half a year to try, and the record of the case is over 18,000 pages long. Necessarily, it will take considerable time for a final decision to be reached. It is unfortunate that this is so, but such a situation is apt to arise in any large plant where numerous allegedly discriminatory charges must be considered.

Be assured that every effort is being made to effect early disposal of his case and that your individual rights will be as carefully protected as those of all others involved.[149]

One of the documents in the NLRB case file on 5-C-1565 relates to the computation of back pay due the fifty-two workers. The intermediate report was cited as stating that there would be extreme difficulty in making the back pay calculation on an individual basis. As a result a lump sum payment plan was agreed upon, based on a formula using the number of vessel contracts in the yard. Madden's final report stated:

The lump sum payment award of $65,000 was finally agreed upon by all parties after considerable discussion in order to allow for any possible error in the foregoing calculations which, it is estimated, would be the amount of back pay due the employees involved if we used the terminal point on which the total employment of the Yard was reduced to 35 percent. It was agreed by all the parties that the payment of the lump sum back pay was the only feasible way to dispose of this matter; any attempt to settle this matter on any other basis would necessitate considerable delay and hearings with its attendant cost, which all the parties were desirous of avoiding.[150]

Of the fifty-two IUMSWA members entitled to back pay, the union was able to locate by the spring of 1946 some forty-six members. Extensive searching was undertaken for the missing eight workers due back pay. By the fall of 1946, two additional members had been located. In the spring of 1947, Earle Shawe, the NLRB regional attorney, contacted the syndicated CBS radio show *The Court of Missing Heirs* program in New York, regarding a nationwide search for the remaining six union members. On April 23, 1947, in a "national manhunt," the plea was made for information concerning the current addresses of Roosevelt McDuffie, Caswell Roper, J.L. Smith, Wallace Brudette [*sic*], William Simmons and the widow of H.M. Lowder, Emma Lowder. Apparently the show had success because on May 2, program director James F. Waters wrote the IUMSWA that he had "nearly 100%" success in locating the "missing heirs." In fact, Waters wanted to interview an unnamed "heir" on his May 7 program of *The Court of Missing Heirs*. If one can take Mr. Waters "100%" figure at face value then the show probably located five of the remaining six persons due settlements. Waters noted that he would call the IUMSWA with the address "trusting the telephone strike was settled," otherwise he would wire and specially deliver the information. Each person due a settlement had to supply the NLRB with a W-4 withholding form before checks could be cut. The $65,000 settlement was divided up into net payable to members as wages of $57,497.90, with social security withholdings of $637.20 and income tax withheld of $6,864.90. The long journey to obtain a semblance of fairness with regard to the bitter struggle for IUMSWA recognition at the North Carolina Shipbuilding was finally over.[151]

The long trail of union activity that started in Wilmington during the summer of 1942 came to an end in the fall of 1946 with the CIO agreeing to settlement of the unfair labor practices case. The North Carolina Shipbuilding Company never admitted any guilt on its part of unfair labor practices. Fifty-one workers received lump sum payments again, for a few years' work at Wilmington, but most had found employment elsewhere by 1947. The only lasting legacy was the hard feeling generated by the long trial. Thirty years later, P.F. Halsey still spoke of the Communist union organizers in the CIO. Had the events at the North Carolina Shipbuilding Company yard been more positive, the future of the CIO in the state might have been different. As it turned out, most workers were not interested in a union in the Wilmington area in the postwar period. The union won NLRB elections at Wertheimer Bag Company, Royster Guano Company, Virginia-Carolina Chemical Company and International Mineral and Chemical Company plants at Wilmington in 1946. The union petitioned for an election at the New Port Terminal (Wilmington Terminal Warehouse).[152]

A CIO witness at the NLRB trial of case 5-C-1565 brought down the house when he stated that he spent "one morning from nine until five in the afternoon" shooting craps. The witness was asked, "While you were holding these special games, did you have any discussion, you and your associates, on the subject of the CIO?" The witness replied, "Not when we were shooting craps." "You say the CIO was never mentioned?" prodded the examiner. "Not when we was in the crap game, no, sir," replied the CIO member, as the Wilmington courthouse rocked with laughter. Many aspects of the union drive at the North Carolina Shipbuilding Company yard were comical. However, the legacy of mistrust and hatred of both union and management ran deep and has remained in the land until today. Generally speaking, blacks and women made greater gains during World War II at the North Carolina Shipbuilding Company yard than pro-union workers.[153]

Throughout the long labor negotiations, the North Carolina Shipbuilding Company continued to produce the needed vessels for the Maritime Commission. While union affairs were hotly debated at the plant, war work went on around the clock. The vessels produced by North Carolina Shipbuilding Company were considered by many to be among the best built during the war.

VI.
Vessels

The North Carolina Shipbuilding Corporation produced some 243 vessels at Wilmington, North Carolina, during the years 1941–46. These vessels were United States Maritime Commission standard types. The most famous, the so-called Liberty ships, were designated type EC2-S-C1 by the Maritime Commission. The North Carolina Shipbuilding Company produced 126 vessels of this class. The other main class, consisting of what were hoped to be postwar merchant vessels, were constructed from standard plans supplied by the Maritime Commission for their type C-2 vessels. North Carolina Shipbuilding Company laid down keels for some 117 vessels of the C-2 types. All of the EC2-S-C1 class vessels were delivered to the Maritime Commission. The C-2 types were delivered to the Maritime Commission, private United States ship owners and the United States Navy.

Some fifty-three vessels were turned over to the navy during the war for conversion to AKA (combat cargo), AGC (headquarters), AE (ammunition supply) and AP (auxiliary troop transport). Thirty-two AKA (Maritime Commission type C2-S-AJ3), eleven AGC (C2-S-AJ1), eight AE (C2-S-AJ1) and two AP (both type C2-S-AJ1 also) vessels were built at the Wilmington yards. While their exterior dimensions were the same, the various C-2 vessels were altered considerably to suit the needs of their individual owners. The many variations in the C-2 design caused considerable construction delays when compared to the speed of assembly of the EC2-S-C1 vessels. Not only were the space layouts of the C-2 vessels different, but they also employed different means of propulsion, further complicating attempts at standardization. Compared to the later C-2, the fabrication problems of the EC2-S-C1 vessels were simple.[154]

The Liberty vessels, because of the quantity produced during the war, were often perceived as being rather small. Both the large numbers produced and the routine launchings by the thousands only served to reinforce this image in the public mind. The EC2-S-C1 was over 440 feet long and had a beam of 56 feet. The vessel drew 27 feet of water and had a displacement of 11,000 tons. Three-cylinder triple expansion engines developed 2,500 horsepower. These engines were turn-of-the-century technology and manufactured by numerous companies because the nation's capacity to produce more modern steam turbine propulsion plants was reserved for needed naval armaments. The Liberty ship had a capacity of about three hundred railroad boxcars (500,245 bales) and was capable of plodding along at eleven knots.[155]

The Liberty ship design developed out of the merger of two radically different designs: the British ocean-class tramp steamer and the Maritime Commission standard C-class vessel. In the prewar years, the Maritime Commission was charged with the task of maintaining the readiness of America's merchant marine. Hopefully by keeping in a state of "preparedness," some of the costly mistakes of the World War I shipbuilding and merchant marine fleet depletion would be avoided. To more or less encourage the expansion of a more modern domestic merchant fleet, the Maritime Commission had produced by 1940 a number of standardized plans for vessel construction. These plans were divided into categories, the major ones being the C-type vessels, which carried cargo, the T type, which were oil tankers, and the P type, which were passenger liners. Three standard C-type vessels were laid out and built. The C-1 type had a deadweight tonnage of 9,075, a capacity of about 270 railroad boxcars (452,430 bales) and a speed of fourteen knots. The C-2 type was designed to weigh 8,794 tons, carry about 320 railroad boxcars (536,828 bales) and make about sixteen knots. The largest type, the C-3, was also the fastest. The first C-3 type built, the USS *Sea Fox*, attained a speed of nearly twenty knots. The C-3 type carried about 440 railroad boxcars (732,140 bales) and a weight of 12,500 tons.[156]

The Maritime Commission experimented with a number of new engineering techniques. The major contributions of the prewar program, according to chairman of the Maritime Commission Admiral Land, were the development of the high-pressure, high-temperature steam turbine propulsion machinery (first used in C-3 vessels) and the various improvements in crew and safety standards. The turbines developed in the C-3 program were later used in the VC-2 (Victory ship) and the AKA program. The improvements in safety came about as a result of the tragic burning of the passenger liner SS *Morro Castle* off the New Jersey coast in September 1934. After the SS *Morro Castle* disaster, American naval architects concentrated on the construction of fireproof vessels. Newly built American ships were constructed almost entirely of nonflammable materials. Metal furniture and fixtures were used in crew quarters and passenger accommodations. Insulated bulkheads and partitions divided the vessels into zones to contain flames, should they occur. The Maritime Commission vessels were also noted for their morale-building crew accommodations. Gone were the traditional dark, damp quarters in the forecastle of the vessel. Maritime Commission–designed vessels provided crew quarters amidships in relatively dry, spacious and well-ventilated comfort. Hot and cold running water as well as mechanical food refrigeration and a modern galley found on commission vessels were unknown even in recent seafaring days. Health standards were also raised by the introduction of a system of modern rat proofing. A major economic boon from a commercial operating viewpoint was the excellent cargo handling facilities found on the C types. Most vessels of the C type carried fourteen or fifteen five-ton booms and one large thirty-ton boom, all worked by electric winches powered from an auxiliary electric generator while in port.[157]

The major construction innovation of the Maritime Commission was the introduction of welding to large merchant vessels. While the first welded coaster of around 150 feet was built in Great Britain in 1920, all-welded vessels were not produced generally until the introduction of the Liberty ship program in 1942. Problems developed in the early welds. Generally speaking, the early welded vessels tended to crack and break up shortly after being put to use. While the breakage of steel plates in heavy weather is not uncommon on large oceangoing vessels, usually these cracks are stopped at the next group of rivets. Unfortunately, in the welded vessels, once a crack started it would continue until often the vessel was split in half. These cracks on all-welded vessels often occurred in calm seas and were due, in part, to the then largely unknown phenomenon of "locked-in stress."

Frequently following a quick cold snap, if any weakness had occurred in the welds or additional locked-in stress had occurred during construction, a crack would develop. In a typical wartime solution to the problem, the Maritime Commission developed "crack arrestors" to prevent further fracturing first, and then secondly looked into the causes of the failures.[158] While the exact causes of the cracks were not discovered until after the war, the crack arresters solved the problem, at least for the war's duration.

The introduction of mass welding into the Maritime Commission building program, however, was an innovation that paid off in the long run. Welding enabled shipbuilders to save considerable weight on the completed vessels, and thereby increased their cargo carrying capacity. At the same time welding was a technique better situated to mass production. Welders could be trained faster than the traditional riveters. A few days in welding school and a new welder was made. Riveters, on the other hand, were scarce. Welding—an innovation in the thirties to save weight on cruisers limited to ten thousand tons by naval treaties—soon became essential to the multiple production techniques of the World War II shipyards that turned out ships with the speed of an assembly line. The main contribution then of the Maritime Commission to the Liberty ship program was that of mass production and design standardization along with improved safety and crew comfort in commission-produced vessels.[159]

The basic design of the EC2-S-C1 was born out of the wartime necessity for a quick, easily constructed vessel upon which considerable design work had already been done. A readily available design was found in the British ocean-class vessels that started with plans brought to the United States by the British Technical Merchant Shipbuilding Mission in 1939. The plans called for the construction of a ten-thousand-ton tramp steamer similar in design to those built in England in the early 1930s. The blunt bow vessels were designed to have a maximum deadweight and speed compatible with fuel consumption economy. The resulting vessels were referred to by some ship designers as mere "powered scows," a foretaste of the criticism to be heaped upon the Liberty design. The ocean-class vessels were greeted in England with little enthusiasm because of the feeling of ship owners that they were again, as in World War I, saddled with a lot of slow and inefficient tonnage. The first of this class of vessels built under the United States Maritime Commission, the SS *Ocean Vanguard*, was christened by Mrs. Emory Scott Land at the Todd-California shipyard on October 15, 1941.[160]

The first large "wave" of merchant ship construction to form a part of the "bridge of ships to the allies" was authorized by President Roosevelt on January 4, 1941. This first wave consisted of some two hundred ships to be delivered in 1942. In the interest of time, the design for the vessels had to be selected from existing plans. The ocean-class vessels, which had been under construction and planning for some time proved an early adaptable plan for the emergency EC2-S-C1 vessels of the Maritime Commission. To indicate that these vessels were not of the "standard" type but an emergency class, the government assigned Liberty ships the designation E. This resulted in the now famous designation EC2-S-C1. The firm of Gibbs and Cox initially attempted to design an alternate plan for the emergency vessels, one more suited to postwar needs, yet easy and fast to construct. Since time was becoming very important, Gibbs and Cox soon concluded, no doubt also due to the press of their other work, that the firm could not prepare alternative plans in time. In addition to the complete writing of new plans, the new vessels would have to be "proven" in one of the model basin tests in order to obtain comparative data with the other designs. There simply was not enough time for all of this to take place and still get the program underway with maximum speed. Largely on the basis of the proven design of the ocean-class vessels, Admiral Land decided to favor this design for the emergency vessels.[161]

A number of changes were made, however, in the British ocean design, some minor, others major in nature. The change most readily observable was that in the superstructure of the two vessels. The British ocean-class vessels had a raised forecastle and poop decks, while the Liberty ship design had one unified central deckhouse located amidships. This central deckhouse provided more protection for the crew in rough weather and also speeded unitary fabrication of the vessel. Other changes were made to facilitate construction. For instance, the weather deck did not have the usual camber to allow water to roll off. Instead the weather deck was flat, again to ease fabrication. Liberty-class vessels in fact had extremely smooth fore decks because of their welded seams and for this reason presented a rather attractive deck picture.

An obvious change in line with American fuel availability was the introduction of oil fuel tanks in Liberty-class vessels rather than the coal bunkers in the ocean-class vessels. This demonstrated the extreme coal dependency of the British for their tramp steamers. The Americans, on the other hand, were quite confident of their worldwide tanker fleet.

The Liberty-class vessels used the standard triple expansion steam propulsion plant used in the ocean-class vessels. By the start of the Maritime Commission program, most if not all of the highly desirable high-pressure steam turbines were requisitioned by the navy. As mentioned, wood was eliminated wherever practical as a fire prevention measure.

Many changes were made in the ocean-class vessels to make the ship more comfortable for the crew. More refrigerated space for crew food, running tap water in crew quarters, cooled tap water in the amidships house and a "slop chest" for the crew were some of the amenities of life provided Liberty ship sailors. At the same time, however, many deviations were allowed from the Maritime Commission's own standards. Selected areas built of non-fireproof materials; the omission of mechanical venting in the engine rooms and holds; oil instead of electric galley and accommodation lights; the lack of fire detection systems; heat insulation in crew quarters and certain navigation equipment—all made the Liberty-class vessels

Drawing of Liberty ship.

inferior according to regular Maritime Commission standards. A number of minor changes were made to eliminate fabrication problems, among them a new type of hawse pipe that allowed mass fabrication of the hawse pipe, yet still assured that the anchor could be lowered and also stowed properly. This simple modification, like many others, was crucial to the success of the Liberty ship program.

In addition to the single amidships house, the Liberty-class vessels had a solid weather deck bulwark instead of the ocean-class chin rail. This made for further safety of the crew during rough weather. The EC2-S-C1 design was "faired" only once in the mold loft of the parent company, the Newport News Shipbuilding and Dry Dock Company. "Offsets of the frames were made and distributed" to the shipyards in the Maritime Commission program. During the wartime construction phases of the Liberty program, additional changes were made to accommodate material shortages. Lighter hatch covers and thinner rolled steel plates were examples of this type of change in the original Liberty ship design. In fact, even the length of the anchor chain varied between early and late EC2-S-C1 vessels. The first peacetime vessels went out with 300 fathoms of chain. Later vessels had this reduced to 240, 210, 135 and finally 75 fathoms. As supplies became tighter, these and other changes were made as a matter of wartime necessity.[162]

The Liberty ship started off under a severe handicap as a result of a remark by President Roosevelt in which he referred to the ship as a "dreadful looking object." *Time* magazine was perhaps the first to call the vessels "Ugly Ducklings." However, the vessels had a rather utilitarian beauty all their own. They were definitely a design from the 1930s, but they were not "ugly." The 126 EC2-S-C1 vessels produced at the North Carolina Shipbuilding yard then were a product of both the Maritime Commission standard design and the British ocean-class vessel.[163]

Early in 1943, the Maritime Commission prepared for the construction of a faster type of cargo carrier, more suited to postwar needs than the Liberty class. This new vessel was designated as Victory class. The Victory-class ships had a length of 455 feet, a beam of 62 feet and a draft of 28 feet. The class had a deadweight tonnage of 10,734, a capacity of about 270 railroad boxcars (453,210 bales) and was capable of making almost seventeen knots. The construction of these faster vessels was in response to shipping and naval pleas for vessels that would be competitive in postwar trade and also capable of faster defense against submarines and bombing aircraft. Shipping interests were quite concerned about avoiding a postwar fleet of aging slow Liberty vessels. In fact, the Maritime Commission did remain more or less stuck with large number of Liberty ships in the postwar period, even though many of these vessels were sold (or simply given) to America's allies to help replace the vessels lost during the war. Buyers were quite scarce after the war. Many Liberty ships went to the breakers, after a brief and often undistinguished service. The most important characteristic of the Victory vessels were that their deadweight capacity should equal that of the Liberty design and that the design speed should equal or exceed fifteen knots. During the design of the Victory ship, it was determined that several shipyards, particularly Bethlehem-Fairfield had ways that were too narrow to permit construction of a Victory vessel having a beam of sixty-three feet. As a result the beam was narrowed to sixty-two feet with subsequent changes in other dimension and a slight effect on the stability of the vessel.[164]

In general the Victory vessels were not significant improvements on the Liberty design, with the exception of speed. In fact, improvements on a large scale were not wanted by Admirals Land or Vickery. The design of the vessels was to "be generally such as to utilize to the greatest possible extent the principles found effective in the production of the present Liberty ship." The Victory ships were planned to have about the same speed as the standard Maritime Commission C-3 types, but to have additional deadweight tonnage. At times in yards such as North Carolina Shipbuilding Company, it is almost impossible to determine when the changeover occurred from C-1 types to Victory design. Most of the literature produced by North Carolina Shipbuilding Company refers to the two designs interchangeably.[165]

The need for additional speed also necessitated the procurement of more powerful propulsion plants for the new vessels. In June 1941, the Maritime Commission had let contracts for building new plants for the manufacture of turbines. As early as May 1942, the General Electric Company had begun delivery of the new turbines. As turbines became available, shipyards were converted from the production of Liberty vessels to the new C-2 type. The first yards converted, Alabama Shipbuilding Company, Marinship and Swan Island Shipbuilding Company, were all employed in producing turbine-powered tankers. As more turbines became available, North Carolina Shipbuilding Company was converted to C-2 production.

USS *Storm King* on trials in Cape Fear River with ad on side for War Bonds, 1944.

After a long hassle with the War Production Board, other shipyards began to receive turbines for their C-2-class vessels. North Carolina Shipbuilding Company, however, had been assured a high priority for obtaining turbines because most of their early Victory models were to be modified for navy use and had to possess high-speed fleet convoy capability, primarily for use in the upcoming Pacific campaign against Japan.

Generally speaking, the Victory class of cargo vessels was similar in appearance to the Liberty class. However, to aid in easy construction, a straight sheer line was adopted and a forecastle was added to make the ship seaworthy. Other changes included strengthening of the welding procedures to prevent the infamous cracking; longer spaced, fewer and heavier frame members; and the elimination of some ballast tanks in the number one hold. In addition, a poop deck house was added to accommodate additional guns, gun platforms and a dispensary. As gunnery action in Liberty convoys had become quite active at times, it was decided to add additional guns on the poop deck. Some 117 vessels of this type were constructed in North Carolina Shipbuilding Company.[166]

All of the C-2 vessels were altered to suit their various owners. Some were constructed to navy specifications, others to special needs of shipping interests. These various modifications reduced the ability of the yard to produce vessels at a uniformly fast pace. As the later vessels were completed, extensive modifications were permitted except for changes in the basic hull and propulsion machinery.

These vessels built for private ship owners, especially those delivered to the Grace Line, contained more refrigerated cargo space. In addition, accommodations were built for fifty-two passengers, along with a swimming pool, enclosed weather decks for passenger recreation, enclosed verandas and dining salons. The last of the vessels of the passenger-cargo type C-2 (or VC-2) built by North Carolina Shipbuilding Company were delivered in the fall of 1946.[167]

In addition to the regular cargo vessels authorized, the Maritime Commission also built a number of auxiliaries for the U.S. Navy to take advantage of "excess capacity" in the shipyards originally created to mass-produce Liberty ships. These vessels varied considerably as to type. They ranged from supply transports (AKA) and large troop carriers (P2) to frigates (S2-S2-AQ1), concrete barges (B7-A2) and large oceangoing tugs (V4-M-A1). These naval contracts were a constant source of frustration to the shipbuilders. In many cases after a C-2 vessel was completed, it would be torn down and rebuilt as a naval auxiliary. In one case a C-2 went through two such major transformations. These constant changes led to worker frustrations and, in one case, revolt. In one shipyard, the workers suspected that the reconversion was just a management scheme to make more money; the workers pledged not to purchase any more war bonds unless the conversions ceased. A congressional hearing was held to investigate the matter. In most cases, it was found that these changes were either military-dictated construction improvements or changes demanded due to enemy action or loss (i.e., lessons learned as a result of combat). Nevertheless, these naval auxiliaries caused considerable trouble for shipyard managers and workers alike. It appears that externally most of the AKA (cargo) and AE (ammo) types were similar in design to the C-2 vessels. The superstructure of the AG (command) and the AP (passenger-troop carriers) types was modified to a considerable extent as indicated by several photographs available of completed vessels under way. The exact changes below the superstructure were not as readily apparent. Changes were made in crew and officer quarters, holds, propulsion machinery, communications and armament to suit navy requirements. Fifty-three of these naval auxiliaries were built at the North Carolina Shipbuilding Company plant on the banks of the Cape Fear River. It would appear from published sources that the North Carolina yard, the first C-2 yard, was also the largest converter of naval C-2 vessels. Some details are known about the modifications to the basic C-2 design that the navy requested. These will be discussed in the later chapter on the peacetime history of the vessels.[168]

After the war, a number remained in active service with commercial ship owners, but most were placed in the Maritime Commission reserve fleet anchored in the Cape Fear River. By the late sixties most of these vessels had been afloat for over twenty years. A few were recalled for the Vietnam conflict, but even these proved too costly to modernize. In the early seventies, most of the great reserve fleets were sent to the breakers. The vessels that had served so well as the tramp suppliers of World War II were no more.[169]

VII.
Sailing into Peace

The postwar years saw many vessels built at Wilmington still on the high seas. The bulk of the 108 emergency ship construction vessels for which we still have records remained afloat well into the 1960s. Initially some twenty-one vessels were torpedoed during World War II. These EC2-S-C1 ships went down in locations such as Barents Sea, Oran, Azores, Dutch Guiana, Durban, Cuba, Paranagua and the Indian Ocean. Four vessels were lost to mines, including one that was lost in 1947 off Rijeka, while another blew up in Finschaven in 1944. Three were sunk with aerial bombs during the war, and three vessels were lost to collisions or weather-related accidents. Two North Carolina Shipbuilding Company vessels formed the invasion breakwater at Normandy. Seventy-nine North Carolina Shipbuilding vessels of this class, most of which remained in the large postwar emergency reserve fleets (a few were sold by the Maritime Commission to private owners), were scrapped in the 1960s and 1970s when the fleets were dismantled. One vessel in this class, Hull number 90 (SS *Walter Hines Page*), completed in April of 1943, was appropriately sunk as a fishing reef off the North Carolina coast at Wachapreague, North Carolina, in 1975. Hull number 152 (SS *Robert F. Hoke*), torpedoed in the Arabian Sea in 1943, was refloated, rebuilt and served for a number of years a Royal Navy training ship in Bombay. Hull number 169 (SS *John Lawson*) was converted in 1947 to a liquefied natural gas carrier—the SS *Beauvais*.[170]

Hull number 1, the SS *Zebulon Baird Vance* was converted into a modern hospital ship, the USS *John J. Meany*, for the U.S. Army from November 1943 to July 1944. The conversion to a hospital ship took place at Bethlehem Steel in Boston. The USS *Meany* transported first wounded soldiers (interestingly, the first soldier loaded aboard was a captured German enlisted man) from Europe to Northeastern ports of embarkation. The *John J. Meany* was named after a native of Jacksonville, Illinois, who was a U.S. Army Air Force flight surgeon who was killed by a land mine in North Africa in March of 1943. Major Meany was killed while making a reconnaissance mission with two pilots near Feriana, Tunisia. After serving most of 1944–45 transporting wounded soldiers, the *Meany* returned to New York in January 1946 and was converted into a passenger vessel and renamed the USS *Zebulon Baird Vance*. The first eastbound voyage of the *Vance* was to transport families of U.S. servicemen on permanent station in Western Europe. The vessel also served as a floating nursery to transport war brides to America. On May 7, 1946, the *Vance* left Le Havre with 369 brides and 57 children in reportedly "excellent condition." The vessel was staffed with army doctors and nurses. Two pre-departure checkups certified that all the

USS *John J. Meany*, builders' photograph, 1945.

babies were in good health. When the vessel docked in New York a number of the babies were sick with what the press dubbed a "mystery epidemic." Six babies from the sailing subsequently died at the U.S. Army hospital at Fort Hamilton (Brooklyn, New York). Many other infants became ill on the voyage but got better upon arrival and survived the outbreak. An army investigation found that despite the fact that the babies had been cleared at Le Havre, many were suffering from poor care and hygiene when they boarded. The report stated that "The outbreak…was due to a filterable virus and spread through contact infection." While some mothers alleged that the arrangements on the *Vance* were "inadequate and slipshod," investigators concluded that the epidemic infant diarrhea that broke out on the voyage was probably caused by unsanitary "bottles, dirty hands, or un-sterilized milk." Even the modern shore hospital at Fort Hamilton was unable to save the infants when their intestines became infected with the rapidly multiplying bacteria. This story was related under the title "Voyage of the Vance," in the June 3, 1946 issue of *Time* magazine. In February of 1947 the *Vance* transported eighty-six special German passengers. These families were traveling to the United States under special U.S. Army escort with secret War Department travel orders. Most of these family heads were chemists and engineers needed in the United States for their knowledge of Nazi weaponry. The *Vance* was placed in the James River Reserve Fleet on December 10, 1948, and went to the breakers in 1970 via the Italian scrap iron company, Cantieri Navali of Genoa. See Appendix III for a list of the passengers of this "special voyage" of the *Vance*.[171]

Of the 115 C-2 vessels for which we have records, some ninety ships were eventually sold to private owners. During the war, fifty-three hulls were sold to the United States Navy for use as combat vessels. Interestingly none of these navy vessels appears according to current records to have been lost to enemy action. One

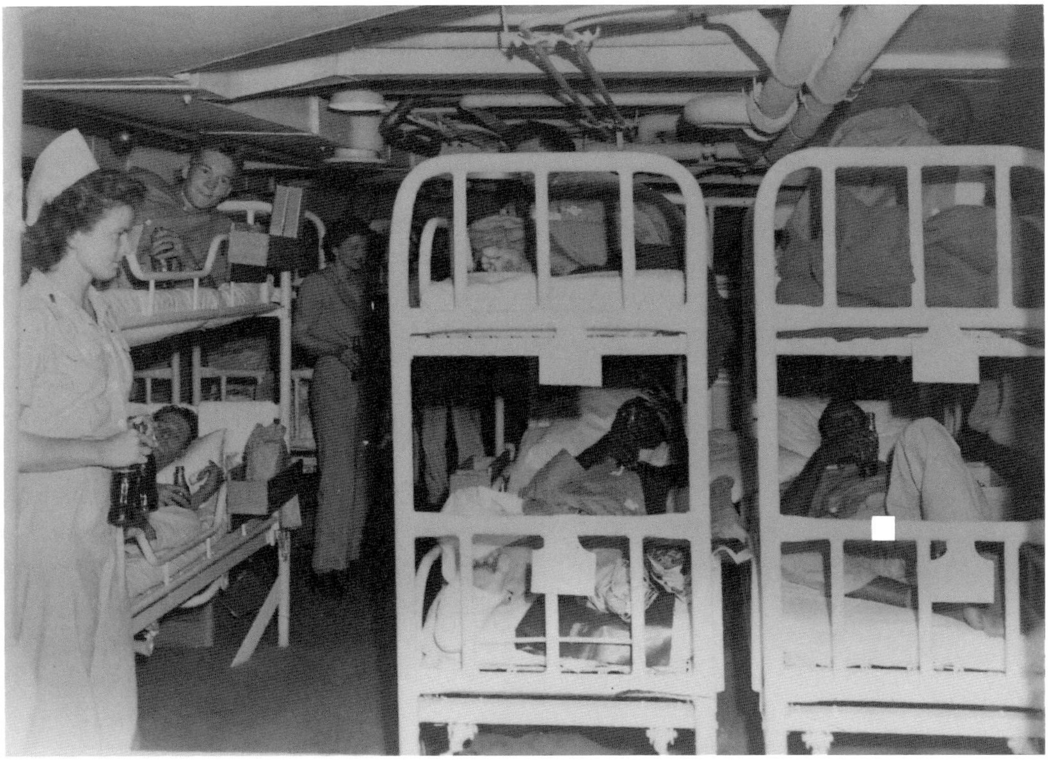

Nurses serve Cokes to wounded servicemen on USS *John J. Meany*, 1946.

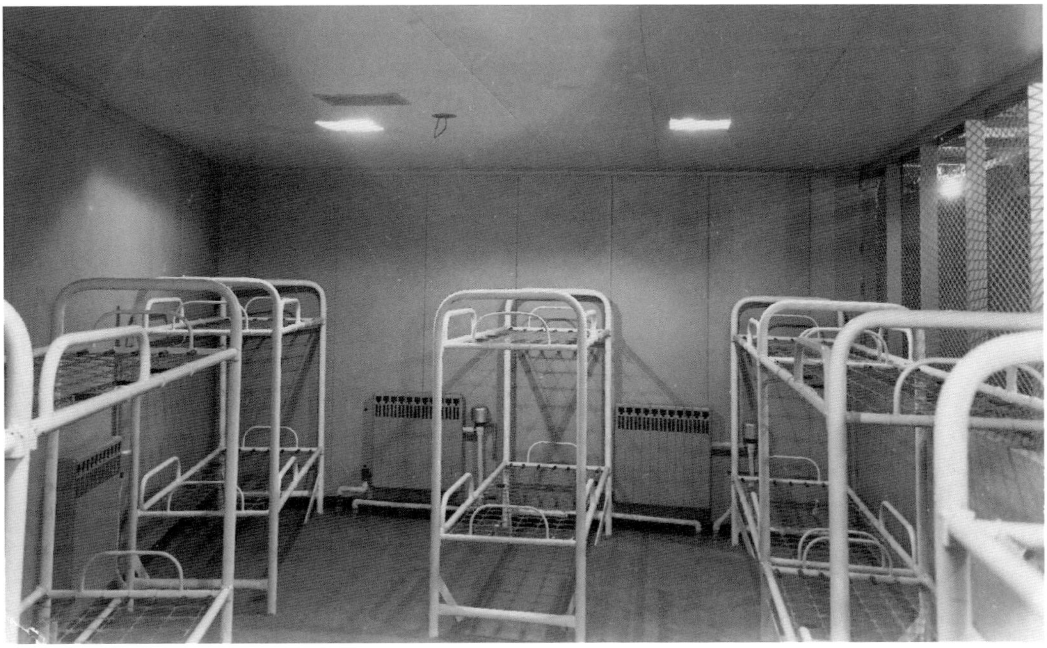

Psychiatric ward on the USS *John J. Meany*, builders' photograph, 1945.

Red Cross worker with wounded serviceman on forecastle, getting sun during westbound Atlantic crossing, USS *John J. Meany*, 1946.

Taking on patients, Europe, USS *John J. Meany*, 1946.

Mrs. Beaman, Red Cross worker and librarian, USS *John J. Meany*, 1946.

USS *John J. Meany* hull at outfitting pier (ex-SS *Zebulon Baird Vance*, hull number 1).

USS *John J. Meany* after outfitting.

USS *John J. Meany* photo of new bridge.

USS *John J. Meany* at outfitting pier.

USS *John J. Meany* at outfitting pier with crane.

ship, hull number 101 (SS *Marco Polo*), was converted into an AE-11-class vessel, the USS *Mount Hood*. The *Mount Hood* was destroyed in a spectacular explosion in the Admiralty Islands in 1944, probably as a result of an accident. Two vessels of the C-2 class remained afloat as late as the 1990s in the U.S. National Defense Reserve Fleets. These were hull numbers 191 and 193, the USS *Vermilion* and the USS *Rankin*, both converted to AKA class vessels for the navy.

Another interesting postwar story involves two vessels constructed on adjacent ways at the Wilmington shipyard, the USS *Midnight* AP 174 (hull number 102) and USS *Starlight* AP 175 (hull number 103). These two vessels, launched on December 23, 1943, were converted in February 1944 to troop transports by the Bethlehem Steel Company yard in Staten Island, New York. The *Midnight* became the SS *Panoceanic Faith* and the *Starlight*, leased in 1948 to the Luckenbach Steamship Company as the SS *Florence Luckenbach*, was sold in 1960 to the State Marine Lines, Inc., and renamed the SS *Badger State*. Both vessels were lost in similar circumstances in the north Pacific during heavy weather on runs to Yokohama during the Vietnam War within two years of each other. The SS *Panoceanic Faith*, carrying a cargo of ammonium sulphate, went down in a matter of minutes on October 9, 1967. The master of the vessel, following a northern route to the Far East, turned south in heavy weather, seeking calmer seas.. The rest of the crew perished when the vessel went down shortly thereafter. There were only five survivors out of a crew of over forty.

The SS *Badger State* was lost in similar circumstances in 1969, carrying poorly loaded air force munitions (500-, 750- and 2,000-pound bombs and claymore mines). The captain of the SS *Badger State*, faced with shifting bomb cargo in the holds broken loose by heavy weather, turned south from his northern route, also seeking calmer seas. Unfortunately, a bomb went off in the number five hold threatening to destroy and sink the vessel. Captain Charles Wilson ordered the life rafts launched and the lifeboats lowered. Again, mechanical problems plagued the launch of the lifeboats, with one being destroyed and the other being dragged alongside the rolling SS *Badger State*. At one point during the attempted breakaway, the full lifeboat passed under the hole in the vessel side made by the explosion. Incredibly, a 2,000-pound bomb that had broken loose from its pallet, rolled out the hole, smashing the lifeboat floating under it and throwing the men in the boat in the forty-eight-degree water. As more bombs started rolling around the sinking vessel, Captain Wilson and the remaining crew jumped in the icy water. Fortunately, a nearby vessel, the SS *Khian Star*, was able to save thirteen of the thirty-nine crewmembers of the SS *Badger State*, including Captain Wilson. The SS *Khian Star* steamed away on the morning of December 27, 1969, leaving the SS *Badger State* a floating danger to navigation. A navy vessel, the USS *Abnaki* shadowed the wreck until it sunk a few days later in a flashes of red, white and orange light.[172]

Immediately following the end of the war some sixty-six vessels of the C-2 class were sold to private shippers. All were initially constructed under Maritime Commission contracts and probably sold at going-out-of-business prices to shippers. These were fast, modern turbine power freighters suitable for worldwide postwar shipping needs. Most of these vessels were scrapped during 1962–79 at the end of their useful lives, having served their owners for sixteen to thirty-three years. Ten vessels of the C-2 class were sold to the Lykes Line (hull numbers 202–203, 208–210 and 225–226) and became the SS *Velma Lykes*, the SS *Louise Lykes*, the SS *Elizabeth Lykes*, the SS *Charles Lykes*, the SS *Stella Lykes*, the SS *Ruth Lykes*, the SS *Tyson Lykes*, the SS *Eugene Lykes*, the SS *Sue Lykes* and the SS *Dick Lykes*. Hulls numbers 117–118, 121, 123, 125, 238–243 were sold to Grace Lines and became the SS *Santa Rita*, the SS *Santa Leonor*, the SS *Santa Catalina*, the SS *Santa Ines*, the SS *Santa Barbara*, the SS *Santa Cecilia*, the SS *Santa Margarita*, the SS *Santa Maria*, the SS *Santa Luisa* and the SS *Santa Isabel*. Grace lines scrapped these vessels in 1968 (SS *Santa Rita*, SS *Santa Catalina*, SS *Santa Margarita*), 1969 (SS *Santa Elisa*, SS *Santa Barbara*), 1970 (SS *Santa Cecilia*, SS *Santa Maria*, SS *Santa Isabel*), and 1973 (SS *Santa Ines*), and 1978 (SS *Santa Leonor*).[173]

Ten North Carolina Shipbulding hulls—numbers 93, 94, 96–99, 101, 108, 196, 198 and 201—were converted to the AGC class: USS *Mount McKinley*, *Mount Olympus*, *Wasatch*, *Auburn*, *Eldorado*, *Estes*, *Panamint*, *Teton*, *Adirondack*, *Pocono* and *Taconic* (the latter three *Adirondack*-class vessels). Interestingly, the *Teton* was

SS *Santa Barbara* at fitting-out pier, 1946.

SS *Santa Isabel* sails past Lady Liberty and Bedloe's Island in New York Harbor, 1946.

the North Carolina Shipbuilding hull 108, SS *Witch of the Wave* (probably laid down on Halloween 1943)! These vessels became AGC 7-17. Of the U.S. Navy conversions a typical postwar story is that of the USS *Pocono* (Hull 198–AGC 16). The USS *Pocono* was an *Adirondack*-class amphibious landing command and control support ship. After completion by North Carolina Shipbuilding in February 1945, the *Pocono* was towed to Boston Navy Yard for fitting out and was commissioned in the navy on December 29, 1945. The shakedown cruise to Guantanamo Bay, Cuba, departed Boston on March 18, 1946, included stops at Key West, Florida and Norfolk, Virginia, ending up in Washington, D.C., on May 7, 1946. For the next few years, the vessel was stationed in the Atlantic Fleet and in early 1948 became the Atlantic Fleet Flagship of Admiral H.P. Blandy.[174]

In addition to air-conditioned quarters for flag officers, the vessel was equipped with complete photographic and printing facilities needed to support amphibious landings. The vessel also had expanded sickbay, radio, radar and communications compartments. Due to the extra weight carried above deck (some say all the brass aboard), the superstructure of the *Adirondack*-class vessels was constructed of a lightweight magnesium alloy. It was hoped that the weight reduction would serve to increase the stability of the vessel, both for the comfort of the crew and to assist with providing a stable base for the photographic, printing and communication platforms. Eleven tons of York air-conditioning equipment provided cooling for the print shop, Radio One, the Combat Information Center (CIC), and the flag officers' quarters. A helicopter-landing pad was added to the stern of the *Pocono*.[175]

After a brief period in 1949–50 in the Atlantic Reserve Fleet, the *Pocono* was recalled from reserve status to again serve as the flagship of the commander, amphibious force, Atlantic Fleet, on which duty she served until 1956. During the Suez crisis in the fall of 1956, the *Pocono* became the flagship of the commander in chief, eastern Atlantic and Mediterranean. In 1957 the *Pocono* served in Operation Deepwater off the coast of Turkey. In 1958 she took part in Operation Packard X amphibious exercise off Onslow Beach, North Carolina. An International Naval Review was held in Norfolk, Virginia, in June of 1958, and the *Pocono* was chosen to again to be the flagship of the commander-in-chief, Atlantic Fleet, Admiral Jerald Wright. Some thirty-three ships and twenty thousand officers and men from all over the world took part in the review. Cyd Charisse was named "Sweetheart of the Navies" for the festivities. From June of 1958 until March of 1959, the ship provided command and control facilities for U.S. forces operating off Beirut, Lebanon, during the political crises in the Middle East. During 1960 and 1961, the *Pocono* participated in amphibious exercises in the Mediterranean and Caribbean.[176]

The *Pocono* was overhauled in Norfolk in early 1962 and departed again for the Mediterranean on July 23, 1962. She was recalled to Norfolk during the Cuban Missile Crisis, where she carried the flag of the commander, amphibious forces, Atlantic. There is some evidence that the *Pocono* was part of the task force that shadowed Soviet vessels during the crises. One former sailor relates the ship being in San Juan following a Caribbean cruise during this period. In any case, she remained at the ready in Norfolk during the remainder of 1962 and 1963. In 1964 she returned to North Carolina to participate in landing exercises at Onslow Beach. In October of 1964 the *Pocono* was deployed to Huelva Bay, Spain, where she participated in Operation Steel Pike I. It was at this point that she became involved in yet another saga of the Gator Navy.[177]

The Gator Navy is a nickname for the amphibious forces in the navy particularly the amphibious force, U.S. Atlantic fleet, which was chronicled in a publication entitled the *Gator*. When the *Pocono* began operations for Steel Pike I, Vice Admiral John S. McCain Jr. (father of U.S. Senator John McCain) was presented as a practical joke with "'Spike', a 2 foot [baby] Alligator, complete with a spike collar and leash." Spike required a special sea detail "to walk around the flag bridge" and feed him in his outfit. Information on Spike was released only on a "strict 'need to know' basis." One sailor related that during the voyage they spotted and picked up an octopus. The officer of the deck, however, was afraid that Spike and the octopus would not get along and ordered the latter thrown overboard. Following the conclusion of Operation Steel Pike I, Spike was returned to the Okefenokee Swamp and all evidence of his journey to the Mediterranean was removed from the *Pocono*. Late November 1964 saw the Pocono at berth at Norfolk. In May of 1965, the *Pocono* departed for the Caribbean and operations of Santo Domingo to aid the U.S. mission during the crises there. She steamed in the area through early 1968 and continued to operate out of Norfolk until she was decommissioned in September of 1971. She was struck from the navy rolls five years later in December of 1976 and went to the breakers in New York (Union Minerals and Alloys) on December 3, 1981.[178]

Another AGC-class vessel the USS *Estes* (AGC-12, hull number 98, SS *Morning Star*) has a similar story to the *Pocono*. The *Estes* was launched on a Sunday—November 1, 1943—an unusual event and often one that mariners considered unlucky. The *Estes* was completed and transferred to the navy in February of 1944. She saw service as a command and control ship in as the flagship of Task Force 52 in Iwo Jima in February 1945 and in the flagship for Task Force 52 in the assault on Okinawa during March and April 1945. In late 1945–46 she operated in the Philippines and China as the flagship of Seventh fleet Admiral T.C. Kinkaid and later Vice Admiral D.E. Barbey. Following overhaul in 1947 and reserve status 1949–50, she subsequently participated in the United Nations Korean War offensive of summer and fall of 1951 and in the following 1951–52 winter campaign as the flagship of Admiral I.N. Kiland, commander of the amphibious force of the Pacific. The fall of 1952 also saw the *Estes* take part in nuclear weapons tests in the Marshall Islands. Following a brief assignment as an arctic expedition supply ship in the summer of 1953, the *Estes* resumed duty assisting with the atomic weapons testing in Eniwetok. In 1955 the *Estes* helped with the evacuation of civilians from North Vietnam, operating as a command and control ship from in the port of Haiphong from August 18 to October 29 of that year following the withdrawal of French forces from Indochina. The vessel continued to assist with amphibious operations and exercises in the Far East during the period 1954–63, including joint exercises with the Royal Navy and the Royal New Zealand Navy.

Following a period of continued voyages in the Far East in the early 1960s, the *Estes* next assisted with amphibious assault duties in Vietnam War during 1965–1968. She served in the Vietnam Defense Campaign of 1965, the Vietnam Counteroffensive Phase II (1966), Phase IV (1968) and Phase V (1968) and the Tet Counteroffensive of early 1968. The summer and fall of 1969 saw the *Estes* end her service to the navy. On January 1, 1969, she had her designation changed to LCC-12 (in 1969 all amphibious vessels were renamed with the L class designation), and she was decommissioned on October 31, 1969, when her duties were turned over to a more modern class of amphibious command and control operations vessels. She remained in the National Defense Reserve Fleet until December of 1977 when she was sold by the United States Maritime Administration (MARAD) for scrap.[179]

Another North Carolina ship, the USS *Rankin* (AKA-103, hull number 193) had a similar tale as the two prior vessels. The *Rankin* is a *Tolland*-class, fast-attack cargo ship that was launched on December 22, 1944. Acquired by the navy in January 1945, following fitting out at the Charleston Navy Yard, the vessel departed in the company of USS *Tollberg* (APD-103) for the Canal Zone. After a transit of the canal, the *Rankin* headed to San Francisco where she took on 5,000 tons of ammunition. She next headed to Okinawa to join Task Force 52 in the assault on the Japanese-held island. Departing Okinawa on June 28 for Saipan in a convoy, the *Rankin* next headed independently for San Francisco where she arrived July 20, 1945. She next took on a load of landing craft, which she subsequently delivered to the Philippines. In the

Philippines, she took onboard the Twenty-fifth U.S. Army Division and transported it to Honshu, Japan, where it embarked on October 27, 1945. The *Rankin* next sailed again for San Francisco where she was decommissioned on May 21, 1947, and placed in the Pacific Reserve Fleet.[180]

The *Rankin* was recommissioned at the Todd Shipyard in Alameda on March 22, 1952, for service in the Korean conflict. Her assigned port was Norfolk, where during the period 1952–58, she assisted the Atlantic Fleet in amphibious operations along the East Coast, Caribbean and Mediterranean. In 1958 she was also part of the Sixth fleet force that landed five thousand U.S. Marines on the shores of Beirut, Lebanon. From 1959 onward, the *Rankin* was back at Norfolk with the Amphibious Squadron Ten operating in the Caribbean and calling on Puerto Rico, U.S. Virgin Island, Haiti, Jamaica and Cuba. In 1962 it saw operations as part of the U.S. response to the Cuban Missile Crisis, and in 1963 the *Rankin* assisted the Second Marine Battalion in the Dominican Republic. The same year she also headed for Haiti where she remained for thirty-one days until tensions eased. In 1964 the *Rankin* headed east to the Mediterranean for Operation Steel Pike I. In 1965 the *Rankin* returned to Dominican Republic waters to assist with the evacuation of over a thousand political refugees and United States nationals. As a result of this operation with other vessels in what was called "PhibRon 10," the *Rankin* received a Navy Unit Commendation from President Lyndon Baines Johnson. October 1966 saw the *Rankin* again in the Caribbean, this time of the shore of Haiti, providing disaster assistance to victims of Hurricane Inez. Food, medical supplies and building materials were transported to help with the rebuilding of damage on the island.[181]

After a refit in 1967 the *Rankin* returned to her duties with Amphibious Squadron Ten. A spring and summer 1968 cruise visited San Juan, Cuba, Panama, the U.S. Virgin Islands, Aruba and Jamaica. Late summer 1968 saw the Rankin part of exercise called "Riverine 68," which demonstrated Marine capability in "combating jungle warfare" (read: Vietnam). In November of 1968, the *Rankin* was assigned to help with the secondary recovery of the Apollo 8 moon orbital flight capsule at the backup site off Bermuda. The vessel was reclassified as LKA-103 (as mentioned amphibious craft were assigned classifications beginning with the letter L) on January 1, 1969, and she spent the rest of the years 1969–70 on supply duty on the East Coast, Caribbean and Mediterranean. In February of 1971, she was decommissioned and on July 24, 1988, sunk as an artificial fishing and diving reef off the coast of Stuart, Florida.[182]

VIII.
Close of the Yard

The postwar history of the yard is nearly as controversial as the selection of the initial site. It became an almost endless battleground between the North Carolina Ports Authority and the United States Maritime Commission. The last vessel built at the yard, the SS *Santa Isabel*, was launched on April 16, 1946. This brought to an end five years of the North Carolina Shipbuilding Company. It left idle a $20-million facility, which at its peak employed some 25,000 people. The immediate impact of the yard closing, together with the loss of other defense plants in the area, combined with the mass influx of returning veterans produced an economic collapse in the Wilmington area. One of the solutions offered to end this economic stagnation was the creation of a North Carolina state port and a ship rework yard at Wilmington.

The yard would, it was hoped, provide an immediate economic shot in the arm by employing large numbers of unemployed veterans and shipyard workers. Equipment and facilities at the North Carolina Shipbuilding Company yard would be combined with a dry dock facility. The main task of this new yard would be the reworking of and overhaul of war-produced shipping. In short, the new yard would bring old Liberty- and Victory-class cargo vessels up to modern postwar maritime standards. At the same time, a facility would be constructed that would provide a port terminal for goods imported to and exported from the Tar Heel state. Most of the shipbuilders formerly employed by the North Carolina Shipbuilding Company would be employed in the rework facility, while veterans could be expected to find work along the state docks.

This idea was not new to the Wilmington area. With little success, the same scheme had been tried at the end of World War I. In 1922 the U.S. Shipping Board had turned over to the city of Wilmington, a large area to the north of the North Carolina Shipbuilding Company site. This area had been used by the U.S. Emergency Fleet Corporation to construct vessels during the war. A clause was inserted in the deed that the property would revert to the federal government if "Port Facilities" were not erected by the city of Wilmington within ten years. The city was unable to erect the facilities in the time allotted, even though the city fathers applied for two successive five-year extensions for completion of the requirements. At some point early in World War II, the City of Wilmington sold the U.S. Emergency Fleet Corporation site to a number of "industrial corporations," despite the fact that the city did not have clear title to the land. In the press of war defense work, matters such as clear title were often overlooked. The Maritime Commission decided correctly that it was more important to construct the ships first, then worry about who owned the land later. This was the case with the old U.S. Emergency Fleet Corporation's site. As late as 1949, at least one of the concerns located on the site of the World War I yard was still trying to obtain a clear title to its land "purchased" from the City of Wilmington.[183]

Roger Williams stated on November 10, 1945, that the Maritime Commission was "scouting around right now for a suitable dry dock" (presumably a floating dry dock facility) for the Wilmington rework yard. The shipyard hoped also to receive contracts for preparation of vessel lay up and anchorage, and for continued repair and maintenance of stored ships.[184] Representative J. Bayard Clark next announced on February 6, 1946, that the sum of $20 million was "likely" to be utilized by North Carolina Shipbuilding Company to "re-convert certain classes of ships not to be declared surplus." Clark stated that no new construction would be given to Wilmington or any other yard under the Maritime Commission's peacetime program. That same day it was announced that the Maritime Commission had submitted a plan to Congress, with the U.S. Surplus Property Administration recommending that the Wilmington facility "be retained as a permanent shipbuilding and repair yard."[185]

Unfortunately for Wilmington, a new dry dock proposal in the spring of 1946 ran against the postwar hopes of the Newport News Shipbuilding and Dry Dock Company of Virginia. Newport News Shipbuilding did not need in the lean postwar years a competing dry dock a few hundred miles to the south. To look after company interests in Wilmington, a former North Carolina Shipbuilding Company official, P.F. Halsey, was placed on the Wilmington Port Commission to keep an eye on things in Wilmington.[186] What Newport News Shipbuilding needed to do was to get the Wilmington yard placed in a limbo status. The yard would ideally neither be a competing shipyard run by the state of North Carolina nor a facility run by Newport News Shipbuilding. Fortunately for Newport News Shipbuilding, the Maritime Commission came up with the required limbo status—a reserve shipyard status for the North Carolina Shipbuilding Company's facilities. While the federal government declared that it had no plans for immediate future use of local yards, it did plan to keep four yards in a reserve status. Three of these yards were on the West Coast, the fourth and only one on the Atlantic Coast was the North Carolina Shipbuilding Company facility at Wilmington, North Carolina. About forty persons would be retained to look after "the interests of the Company," the commission announced.[187]

As early as July 1946, some three months after the launch of the last vessel, the North Carolina Shipbuilding Company site had been selected by the Maritime Commission for use as its eastern seaboard reserve yard. The North Carolina yard was selected because of the yard's "ability to build standard size ships of moderate size, efficiently laid out, of sufficiently permanent construction to withstand deterioration for a considerable period, and it is anticipated that there will be available personnel and management of the nearby Newport News Shipbuilding to draw upon in any future emergency."[188] The yard's proximity to the large reserve fleet lying at anchor in the Cape Fear River also played an important role in its selection as a reserve yard.[189] When it turned over the yard to the Maritime Commission, the North Carolina Shipbuilding Company ended its interest in a "rework" facility at Wilmington.

In November 1946, Ronaldo B. Page and the North Carolina congressional delegation petitioned the Maritime Commission for use of the yard.[190] The plan was to pay $1.2 million for the facility. A portion of the yard would be devoted to "the repair of ships," with the balance being a state port. The memo to the Maritime Commission pointed out economic loss in waterfront facilities, employment and shipping had occurred because of the war, emphasizing the "the Port of Wilmington has been in the fullest sense a war casualty."[191] Nevertheless, the Maritime Commission rejected this proposal on December 15, 1946.[192] The commission stated, "In the view of the unsettled international situation, the Commission feels that…it must, in the interest of national security, maintain its four reserve shipyards in proper stand-by condition, and therefore could not grant permission to the State of North Carolina to use this property."[193]

Wilmington interests attempted during the course of 1946 and 1947 to use the offices of North Carolina's elected representatives in Washington to expedite the transfer of the yard to the state. Memos were addressed to Governor R. Gregg Cherry; Senators Josiah W. Bailey and Clyde R. Hoey; and Representatives Herbert C. Bonner, John H. Kerr, Graham Q. Barden, Harold D. Colley, John H. Folger, Carl T. Durham, J. Bayard Clark, Jane Pratt, Robert L. Doughton, Sam J. Ervin, Albert L. Bulwinkle and Zebulon Weaver in late November 1946.[194] On February 27, 1947, Representative Clark had a conference with William W. Smith of the commission and John R. Steelman, special assistant to President Truman. As a result of this conference the Maritime Commission again gave a "thorough consideration" to the matter.

On January 31, 1947, Steelman announced to the assembled North Carolina delegation that he would conduct a complete and thorough investigation into the status of the North Carolina yard at Wilmington before reporting to President Truman. United States Senator William B. Umstead reported that "Mr. Steelman indicated a real interest" in the matter. The delegation asked the president to hold up "any disposal of equipment…until the entire matter is satisfactorily finished." President Truman was reported to have told the North Carolinians that Steelman would "investigate in detail before any final action is taken."[195]

Steelman called the North Carolina congressmen back for a "joint meeting to thrash out the differences if possible," on February 27, 1947. Senator Hoey maintained, "Steelman is really anxious to help us." The North Carolina delegation reported that it had made "progress" in its joint conference with advisor Steelman and Maritime Commissioner William W. Smith. An additional meeting was scheduled early in March, but no definite date was set. The delegation remained "hopeful" that an agreement would be reached in regard to the yard offer.[196]

On March 19, 1947, William W. Smith of the Maritime Commission informed Representative Clark that, primarily for national defense reasons, the commission would not declare the Maritime North Carolina yard surplus "either at this time nor in the foreseeable future."[197] Clark, in a cable to Governor Cherry, related that the recent "letter for the Maritime Commission at all means the views of Mr. Steelman who fully understands the situation and appreciates the need in our state for more adequate facilities…In my judgment Steelman will make a favorable recommendation to the President unless the Maritime Commission can present some need that I have not yet been able to see."[198] All of this not so subtle clubbing apparently for the moment left the Maritime Commission unmoved.[199]

On March 27, 1947, Senator Hoey was again reassured by Presidential Assistant Steelman that a "further investigation would be made." One can only wonder what "further investigations" were made with the Newport News Shipbuilding and Dry Dock Company.[200]

R.B. Page later reported on November 27, 1947, that he was working "out several differences with the Commission." This time John R. Steelman promised he would "iron out the differences of opinion" if the North Carolina delegation failed to reach agreement with the Maritime Commission. Charleston, Savannah and Norfolk had received shipyards from the commission. Some eighty-seven ships had been assigned to the Todd shipyard in Charleston for overhaul, Page related: "These ships were originally scheduled to be overhauled at Wilmington." One can only assume that the same Todd Shipbuilding Company would have overhauled these vessels in Wilmington had the facility been available there.[201]

The Maritime Commission meeting on May 7, 1948, however, delayed indefinitely a decision on leasing the yard. Colonel George W. Gillette, executive director of the state ports authority and leading advocate of the *Wilmington Post*, in a statement was still "very hopeful" as always. "The tense international situation [blockade of Berlin by the Soviets]" made the commission "hesitate to lease even a portion" of the yard according to Gillette. Gillette went on to state that he had a luncheon conference "on the subject" with McMahon of Newport News Shipbuilding, who was at the Wilmington yard. Gillette said McMahon was "interested" in plans for installing ship repair facilities and pre-fabricating ship parts at Wilmington.[202]

In a telephone interview from Washington with a reporter for the *Wilmington Star*, Colonel Gillette declared on July 29, 1948, that the commission "had definitely promised the State…a lease on the yard." Gillette continued that "matters of this kind move slowly, and he could not say exactly when the lease would be consummated." Gillette also stated that a "Gulf Coast shipbuilding company" was interested in building and repairing cargo vessels and tankers at Wilmington if the state gets possession of the shipyard. One cannot help but wonder if more conferences in Newport News with McMahon would have speeded the commission along.[203]

In November of 1948, Gillette traveled to Washington with R.B. Page to replead North Carolina's case. Gillette termed the Maritime Commission rental proposal "unreasonable." Commissioner Grenville Mellen and Gillette had some "plain talk" according to the account in the *Wilmington Star*. Perhaps the "plain talk" concerned Newport News Shipbuilding and Dry Dock Company. In other words, if there would be no "Gulf Cost shipbuilder" coming to Wilmington then the state could lease the yard. This time a new proposal from the state called for a working agreement between the state and the Maritime Commission while the technicalities of the contract were smoothed out.[204]

The House Merchant Marine and Fisheries Committee held hearing in early March of 1949 on a Maritime Commission proposal to use a surplus navy floating dry dock to service reserve fleet vessels in the basin at Wilmington. Unfortunately a "private shipyard" spokesman told the Merchant Marine Committee that the proposal to move the dry dock to Wilmington "would be unwarranted government interference with private enterprise." The dry dock would draw away business from shipyards at Charleston (Todd Shipbuilding Company) and Hampton Roads (Newport News Shipbuilding and Dry Dock Company), according to the "spokesmen." The North Carolina backers believed that the dry dock would be an inducement for ships to call at the Wilmington port for repairs and maintenance. Private shipyard "spokesmen" argued that "there was not sufficient ship and overhaul business to justify the risk" of establishing a new repair facility. In other words, the other yards wanted to monopolize all the business. The navy, however, agreed (and well they might since Newport News Shipbuilding and Dry Dock Company was a prime navy contractor) to move the dry dock to Wilmington only if the state of North Carolina would agree to maintain the dock. The navy dry dock cost some $25,000 a year to insure, $15,000 a year for maintenance and would require $250,000 worth of repairs before it could be placed in operation. Wilmington interests were unable to obtain funds from the legislature for setting up this gift horse at Wilmington. If there were no funds, there would be no dock. No dock, no more problem with the "private shipyard spokesmen."[205] During the period a dry dock facility was under consideration, vigorous efforts were underway to secure the North Carolina Shipbuilding Company yard for the North Carolina State Ports Authority.

Ronaldo Page, publisher of the *Wilmington Star*, is generally considered to be the "Father of the North Carolina State Ports Authority." Page was an advocate of state funding of deep-water ports for both Wilmington and Morehead City. From the 1930s until his death in 1955, he was instrumental in securing a modern port facility for North Carolina. Using his newspaper in Wilmington, Page hoped to promote "a movement for better seaports and for returning the state to its former position in world commerce."[206]

Page began his campaign for the location of a North Carolina State Ports Authority in the mid-1930s. He was eventually successful in securing a long-term postwar lease from the Maritime Commission. He began negotiations with the Morehead City Port Commission in 1937 for facilities there. He was instrumental in obtaining as Works Progress Administration grant to study the type of facilities needed. Page was an original member of the port authority and was elected its first chairman. Another Wilmington man, Cyrus Hogue, an attorney, prepared the legislation for the ports authority.[207]

The act in 1945 that created the North Carolina State Ports Authority did not provide funds, but rather initially relied on Federal Works Agency advances for funding. In the post–World War II period, the Works Progress Administration had been morphed into a new part of the Truman administration, the Federal Works Agency. The agency had the authority to handle all postwar government building contracts in the continental United States. The authority was empowered to apply for and accept loans and grants from federal agencies and the state of North Carolina. In June of 1946 the authority asked the Council of State for $25,000 annually to supplement the Federal Works Agency grant. An appropriation of $50,000 was made for the biennium 1947–48 for the purpose of preparing preliminary plans. This included acquiring a site for the port, making a statewide survey of shipping needs and the drawing up of plans for a state port "comparable to any other port on the South Atlantic Coast."[208]

The original board of directors of the North Carolina State Ports Authority was appointed in 1945 and consisted of seven members who served until 1949. In March 1949, all seven members resigned to enable Governor W. Kerr Scott to enlarge and appoint nine members of his choosing. Of the seven original members only two served on the new Scott-created board. In 1953 William B. Umstead reduced the board back to seven in number. Umstead also reappointed only two of the previous board members. The Umstead board expired in 1957 and Governor Luther Hodges, dissatisfied with the policies of the authority did not reappoint a single member. The authority was restructured in 1961 by the legislature so that each new governor was to appoint a new full board when he enters office. One of the first acts of the original 1945 board was the start of negotiations with the U.S. Maritime Commission for a lease on the northern extension of the North Carolina Shipbuilding Company site.[209]

Actual plans with the Maritime Commission for building a postwar state port facility at Wilmington go back to late 1945. On November 10 of that year, Admiral Howard L. Vickery, vice-chairman of the Maritime Commission came to Wilmington on an inspection tour. During the tour, Roger Williams, president of North Carolina Shipbuilding Company, outlined the area on the Cape Fear River to be dredged out for a "storage basin for surplus American Merchant ships." The area, to be dredged deep enough for Liberty-class vessels (C-2), went from the southern tip of Eagle's Island, where the Brunswick River joins the Cape Fear River, to the U.S. Highway 17 bridge over the Cape Fear River. North Carolina Shipbuilding Company received the contract for dredging in the storage basin area.

Major General Philip Fleming of the Federal Works Agency, according to Representative Clark, on February 26, 1946, announced that the North Carolina State Ports Authority would receive a grant of $90,000 to prepare plans and specifications for improvements to the Wilmington port. Improvements recommended included 35,000 linear feet of shoreline bulkhead, 1.5 million yards of dredging, the building of new roads and five miles of railway track. Transit sheds of 477,000 square feet of tobacco storage and miscellaneous improvement, structures and equipment were projected. The funds were provided for under Title V of the War Mobilization and Reconversion Act of 1944, which had been passed by Congress to "help cushion the unemployment shock" of the postwar period.[210]

On May 8, 1946, a proposal was submitted to the Maritime Commission by Representative J. Bayard Clark, Governor Cherry, R.B. Page and ports authority counsel ex-Governor Melville Broughton. This memo requested that the commission transfer the North Carolina Shipbuilding Company property and facilities to the North Carolina State Ports Authority. According to Page's newspaper, the *Star*, the Maritime Commissioners John Carmody and Raymond S. McKeogh "reacted very favorably" to the proposal. Governor Cherry reported that the state was prepared to spend $1 million on the project, this amount to be raised via state bonds. The governor argued that this arrangement would save the federal government $25,000 a month in maintenance costs. The proposal to the Maritime Commission was unveiled at a luncheon of the North Carolina Congressional Delegation in Wilmington.[211]

Broughton stated that the ports authority would develop the north yard area, utilizing the outfitting wharves as piers for the port, leaving the nine main shipways for Maritime Commission reserve use. Governor Cherry stated that this was "the one great chance for the state to develop a real state port."[212]

In May 1946 and again in August, the ports authority under the chairmanship of R.B. Page had addressed a memorial to the Maritime Commission outlining the need for improving the economy of the area by the construction of a state port out of the "surplus" Wilmington yard. The Maritime Commission had been auctioning off other wartime yards throughout the country to the private sector. Here was an ideal opportunity for the government to grant large facility for the economic improvement of the Wilmington region. The Maritime Commission was unimpressed by this proposal, however. They rejected the ports authority's offer primarily on the ground that the yard was currently designated a reserve facility. The minutes of the Maritime Commission also reveal, however, that the fate of the World War I yard was also in the minds of the commissioners. They noted that the earlier yard had in fact been sold by a local government (Wilmington) to the private sector. The Maritime Commission felt that it was its duty to see that the same fate did not befall the valuable North Carolina Shipbuilding Company yard.[213]

When contracts for vessel construction had been completed after World War II, the yards, which were operated on a rent-free lease basis by the private shipbuilding companies, again became the custody of the Maritime Commission. When this occurred the name of the yard changed to the Maritime North Carolina yard and came under custody of Real Estate and Terminal Division of the Maritime Commission.[214]

R.B. Page of the North Carolina State Ports Authority announced on August 29, 1947, that "tentative agreements" had been made with the Maritime Commission to lease a part of the North Carolina Shipbuilding Company yard. The ports authority had offered to pay one dollar a year on a ninety-nine-year lease for "100 acres of land, 3,000 feet of waterfront, one large prefabricated building and several small structures," on the northern extension of the yard. J. Melville Broughton reported that the Maritime Commission was holding out for three successive twenty-five year leases at a yet-to-be-agreed-upon figure. Page stated that the agreement would be sent in a memo from the commission in a day or two. After the ports authority approval, the commission would then draw up a lease.[215]

Broughton went on to say: "This means that a lease agreement definitely will be made…we have virtually reached an agreement on all details of the lease and from all indications the final papers will be drafted and signed within 15 days." He claimed that the best estimate of the federal and state expenses would "run close to 50/50 for development of the $5-million yard. The agreement came with "dramatic suddenness." The commission had rejected earlier proposals outright. "We noted a pleasant change of attitude on the part of the commission's representatives," Broughton explained with a smile. The former governor related that the clincher was the ports authority's willingness to contract facility improvements. The results of a study by Harris Engineering Company of New York, outlining improvements projected by the state was presented along with the latest proposal before the Maritime Commission. Advisor Steelman suggested to President Truman that the commission should not sell nor give the yard away, but rather should work out a lease agreement.[216]

On October 31, 1947, the ports authority rejected the Maritime Commission offer of a seventy-five-year lease on the northern part of the yard. The authority would not agree to the following commission requirements: The state was to pay 5 percent of all gross receipts annually, while the state wanted 5 percent of the net receipts after expenses. Payment on the receipts was to start when improvements were completed, according to the commission proposal; the state, however, did not want to pay until after the improvements were paid for. The Maritime Commission also wanted the power to veto any "marine-related" industry brought in the area. The ports authority wanted a free hand to bring in all industries of any type. The commission also wanted to decide whether the property was maintained according to Maritime Commission standards or not, while the state wanted only to guarantee the present condition of the yard subject to "reasonable wear and tear."[217]

Colonel Gillette announced in a Wilmington Cape Fear Club meeting held on February 26, 1948, that he was hopeful that the North Carolina State Ports Authority would reach an agreement with the Maritime Commission in the next "30 days." On March 19, Gillette stated in Washington after talking with Howard Marsden of the Maritime Commission's Real Estate Division that the commission would act in two or three more weeks, on the ports authority's "final offer to lease the North portion of the yard." Under the new proposal, the commission would reserve the right to inquire into the state's "intention for shipyard development," if at the end of five years sufficient improvements had not been made. The commission would also lease unneeded equipment from the remainder of the yard to the ports authority, and in the event of war, the commission would allow the state to continue to use the leased portion of the yard.[218]

In June, another meeting was held in Washington with Page, representatives of the Maritime Commission, the North Carolina Congressional Delegation and Presidential Advisor Steelman all attending. Page stated on June 17, 1948, that prospects "look pretty favorable." J. Bayard Clark reported that the commissioners seemed "much more interested and somewhat favorably inclined." Clark Hoey said they were "very receptive." W.B. Umstead responded that he "expected a decision fairly promptly." The ports authority needed an answer so funds could be requested in the 1948–49 state budget.[219] Almost a year later the Maritime Commission and the ports authority were still working out the details of a contract.

A working agreement finally formed the base of an accord in the five-year attempt by the North Carolina State Ports Authority to obtain the yard. On March 3, 1949, Joseph K. Carson Jr., a member of the Maritime Commission, stated that a "letter of intent" would be forthcoming on Friday from the commission regarding the yard. With this letter Wilmington advocates would then be able to plead their case for funds to the state legislature in Raleigh. In the March trip, Gillette and Page again conferred with the full commission. Senator Broughton "voiced confidence that the lease is merely a matter of legal negotiation and detail." Commission chairman William W. Smith told Broughton that the commission is "favorably disposed" to a long-term lease.[220]

On November 16, 1949, North Carolina's long cherished dream of a new deep-water port became a reality. The U.S. Maritime Commission signed a lease agreement with the State Ports Authority. As the Newport News Shipyard became assured that there would be no Todd shipyard or dry dock at Wilmington, gradually their attitude toward a potential rival yard changed. In addition, as the cold war need for a reserve yard became less and less a national priority (with the lifting of the Berlin blockade and the easing of U.S.-Soviet tensions) and as costs for maintaining the yard mounted, the Maritime Commission changed its stance. The agreement, signed on November 16, 1949, after some five years of negotiations, called for a fifty-year lease, at one dollar per year, for the northeast (or plate storage) section of the yard. Under the agreement, the Maritime Commission reserved the right in the event of a national emergency to terminate the lease of the North Carolina State Ports Authority. In addition to the Maritime Commission lease, the ports authority purchased an additional twenty-nine acres at $1,000 an acre for future expansion. This was done in order to add to the space that was leased from the Maritime Commission.[221]

Initial news of the agreement of November 16, 1949, the culmination of five years of North Carolina hopes, came from the office of Senator Clyde Hoey. Also instrumental in the final days was Senator Frank Porter Graham, who succeeded the late Melville Broughton in the Senate and carried on the fight for the yard that Broughton had started in 1945 as an attorney for the ports authority. The State Legislature voted $7 milion for the improvement to North Carolina seaports in 1949, $5 million of which was allocated to open the Wilmington facility. Colonel Gillette stated at the time of the announcement that "we are just getting started."

"I am happy that the lease has been signed, sealed and delivered," remarked the exhausted R.B. Page after his long five-year struggle. "The signing of the lease is the turning of the key to development of a State Port in Wilmington," continued Page. This new agreement it would appear, served both the needs of the state for a deep-water port, and of the Maritime Commission for a standby emergency shipyard.[222]

Events, however, would not turn out that way. Courts soon ruled that because the North Carolina State Ports Authority did not actually own the land, it could not use that land to finance revenue bonds for the development of the port. If the federal government had to exercise their "rights" in the event of a national emergency, there would be no land available to compensate the bondholders. This additional logjam in Wilmington's maritime aspirations was cleared up in 1956, when the legislature appropriated funds for the authority to purchase some 323 acres on the west bank of the Brunswick River in Brunswick County that were to be offered to the Maritime Commission in exchange for the entire Maritime North Carolina Yard. In 1961 the North Carolina

State Ports Authority leased an additional 115 acres—most of the remaining Maritime North Carolina site—from the Maritime Commission. In November of that year the commission in conjunction with the navy "decided" that the Wilmington shipyard was no longer necessary for mobilization purposes "and agreed to lease the remainder of the property for ten years at a rental of one dollar a year plus maintenance." After the lease expired in 1971, the state of North Carolina further agreed to purchase the Maritime North Carolina yard for $445,000 plus the cost of the buildings after the lease expires.[223]

It was some twenty-six years after the founding in 1945 of the North Carolina State Ports Authority before all of the Maritime North Carolina yard actually became the property of the State of North Carolina. The facility, which originally was built to construct Maritime Commission vessels, now has become the main entrepôt for the state of North Carolina. Just as the site was ideal for the construction of vessels, it also was a good location for the import and export of goods. The land transportation facilities that enabled the North Carolina Shipbuilding Company to construct vessels in record time, now speed the foreign commerce of North Carolina to and from the state through the port of Wilmington.

Some of the vessels built at Wilmington, however, remained afloat to engage in this commerce, until the end of the twentieth century. A number of North Carolina Shipbuilding Company–constructed vessels also made up the Maritime Commission Reserve Fleet that was anchored in the Cape Fear River and at other reserve fleets. All of these vessels have now been scrapped. The vessels built in North Carolina at Wilmington, no longer serve her on the high seas.

IX.
Conclusion

With war clouds hanging over most of Europe, President Franklin Delano Roosevelt searched for a way to aid his Allies abroad. A continuous supply of war material was a basic necessity in fighting the Axis threat. Getting the material to the front through the German U-boat net that blanketed Europe proved a greater difficulty than the manufacture of the war material itself. Roosevelt commissioned Admiral Emory Scott Land, chairman of the Maritime Commission, to provide a "Bridge of Ships," to the Allies in Europe and the Pacific. North Carolina proved to be a vital link in that bridge. The 243 vessels built by the North Carolina Shipbuilding Company made an important contribution to the war effort. More importantly, emergency shipyards such as the North Carolina Shipbuilding Company enabled the regular navy and established yards to continue with the backlog of orders for battleships, cruisers and carriers. Ultimately, the Maritime Commission emergency yards would also build some of the smaller navy carriers and supply ships. The Maritime Commission soon found that establishing an average emergency shipyard such as North Carolina Shipbuilding Company was no easy task. Local interests, politics and party loyalties often played a role in site selection, operation and even eventual shutdown of the emergency yards.

The brief life of the North Carolina Shipbuilding Company was surrounded by controversy. The yard was born amid a dispute between Morehead City and Wilmington over the site. Newport News Shipbuilding and Dry Dock Company stepped in and opened a yard in Wilmington, thereby dashing the hopes of rival Morehead City forces. Obtaining adequate labor was an immediate task of the organizers of the North Carolina shipbuilding yard. Throughout the opening days of World War II, Wilmington grew at a very rapid pace. Housing, transportation and adequate materials were always constant headaches for the young company. Workers at the yard soon became embroiled in a bitter dispute over CIO union representation. A major National Labor Relations Board hearing, with unfair labor practices allegations against the maturing management marred most of the years of the company's history. After the completion of some 243 vessels in its demise the yard became the center of another heated controversy. The transfer of the shipyard to the North Carolina State Ports Authority again raised the partisanship of local interest, politics, regional and state loyalties. Newport News Shipbuilding and Dry Dock Company played an important part in the end of the yard as it had in its birth. When Newport News Shipbuilding was assured that an expanded state port at Wilmington would not be either a threat to the shipbuilding industry or railway interests in Virginia, only then did the Chesapeake Bay yard allow the Maritime Commission to lease the yard to the North Carolina State Ports Authority.

The North Carolina Shipbuilding Company had a very profound impact on the city of Wilmington. The sleepy post-Depression coastal town was transformed into a major state industrial center. Wilmington did not go the way of Bath or Woodstock, North Carolina. Wilmington, the state's largest town until the rise of the Piedmont industrial centers in the twentieth century, again found a large place on the map. Wilmington was able to rejoin these industrial centers largely because of the boost the North Carolina Shipbuilding Company and other war industries gave the town. The yard employed workers from throughout the Southeast. Workers came into Wilmington during the war and stayed after the war to work in new postwar industries. They watched some of the same ships they helped build, ride at anchor in the Maritime Commission reserve yard in the Cape Fear River. The North Carolina Shipbuilding Company played a major role in determining the face and thrust of postwar Wilmington. Just as the vessels built by the yard were an important factor in the Allied victory, the yard itself became a major shaper of Wilmington's role as a state port in the latter half of the twentieth century. The men and women who worked at North Carolina Shipbuilding were participants in a global struggle against the Axis powers. North Carolina Shipbuilding held Maritime Commission awards for ship construction and many officers and sailors felt the vessels were the best ones built during the wartime period. Some ships remained in service for several decades following the war and were considered essential to national defense through most of the Cold War. The wartime building program was a unique and monumental national effort that we will probably not see again. The employees of North Carolina Shipyard Company were proud carriers of a shipbuilding tradition that has long been a part of the state of North Carolina.

Appendix I
Ships

The North Carolina Shipbuilding Company produced 243 vessels during its brief existence. The following appendix (on pages 102–123) lists each vessel by hull number along with important construction dates, sponsor and final disposition.

APPENDIX I

Hull #	Name of Vessel	Keel Laid	Launch Date	Delivery Date
1	*Zebulon B. Vance*	5.22.1941	12.6.1941	2.17.1942
2	*Nathaniel Greene*	5.22.1941	1.17.1942	3.12.1942
3	*Virginia Dare*	5.28.1941	2.3.1942	3.27.1942
4	*William Hooper*	8.22.1941	2.21.1942	4.7.1942
5	*Daniel Morgan*	9.3.1941	3.8.1942	4.16.1942
6	*Francis Marion*	9.4.1941	3.22.1942	4.27.1942
7	*Charles C. Pinkney*	12.11.1941	5.10.1942	5.28.1942
8	*John Cropper*	1.22.1942	5.17.1942	6.4.1942
9	*William Moultrie*	2.5.1942	5.22.1942	6.11.1942
10	*Thomas Sumter*	2.25.1942	5.31.1942	6.17.1942
11	*Jeremiah Van Rensselaer*	3.10.1942	6.7.1942	6.24.1942
12	*Artemas Ward*	3.24.1942	6.14.1942	6.30.1942
13	*Hugh Williamson*	5.11.1942	7.7.1942	7.24.1942
14	*William R. Davie*	5.18.1942	7.12.1942	7.29.1942
15	*William Gaston*	5.23.1942	7.19.1942	8.5.1942
16	*William A. Graham*	6.1.1942	7.26.1942	8.15.1942
17	*James K. Polk*	6.8.1942	8.2.1942	8.21.1942
18	*Alexander Martin*	6.15.1942	8.16.1942	8.28.1942
19	*Richard Spaight*	7.8.1942	9.11.1942	9.23.1942
20	*Samuel Ashe*	7.12.1942	9.17.1942	9.29.1942

Sponsor	Type	Disposition
Mrs. J.M. Broughton	EC2-S-C1 (Liberty)	Sold private, scrapped 1970
Miss Edith Bailey	EC2-S-C1 (Liberty)	Torpedoed off Oran and beached 1943, TL
Mrs. Elwood Inge	EC2-S-C1 (Liberty)	Mined off Bizerta, 1944, TL but salvaged, scrapped 1948
Miss Helen Clark	EC2-S-C1 (Liberty)	Torpedoed from the air and lost in the Barents Sea 1942
Miss Evelyn Rogers	EC2-S-C1 (Liberty)	Torpedoed and lost off Northern Russia 1942
Mrs. Storer P. Ware	EC2-S-C1 (Liberty)	Scrapped 1967
Miss Margaret McMahon	EC2-S-C1 (Liberty)	Torpedoed and lost off the Azores 1943
Miss Anne LaPorte	EC2-S-C1 (Liberty)	Scrapped 1965
Miss Marjorie Fletcher	EC2-S-C1 (Liberty)	Scrapped 1970
Miss Frances Robeson	EC2-S-C1 (Liberty)	Scrapped 1971
Miss Agnes Morton	EC2-S-C1 (Liberty)	Torpedoed and scuttled off Cape Farewell 1942
Miss Sally Randolph	EC2-S-C1 (Liberty)	Damaged in collision 1944, sunk as breakwater off Normandy and abandoned 1944
Mrs. Richard D. Dixon	EC2-S-C1 (Liberty)	Wrecked 1946, refloated, scrapped 1948
Mrs. E.M. Handy	EC2-S-C1 (Liberty)	Scrapped 1972
Mrs. A.C. Brown	EC2-S-C1 (Liberty)	Torpedoed and lost in the South Atlantic 1944
Mrs. W.W. Walker	EC2-S-C1 (Liberty)	Scrapped 1972
Miss Jane Blewett	EC2-S-C1 (Liberty)	Torpedoed off Dutch Guiana 1943, CTL, scrapped
Miss Louise Hooper	EC2-S-C1 (Liberty)	Scrapped 1963
Miss Carolyn Cross	EC2-S-C1 (Liberty)	Torpedoed and lost off Durban 1943
Miss Shirley Jean Beasley	EC2-S-C1 (Liberty)	Scrapped 1970

APPENDIX I

Hull #	Name of Vessel	Keel Laid	Launch Date	Delivery Date
21	*Benjamin Williams*	7.19.1942	9.23.1942	10.4.1942
22	*James Turner*	7.26.1942	9.29.1942	10.10.1942
23	*Nathaniel Alexander*	8.2.1942	10.4.1942	10.15.1942
24	*David Stone*	8.16.1942	10.10.1942	10.21.1942
25	*Benjamin Smith*	9.11.1942	10.28.1942	11.7.1942
26	*Joseph Hewes*	9.22.1941	3.29.1942	5.6.1942
27	*John Penn*	9.23.1941	4.12.1942	5.11.1942
28	*John C. Calhoun*	10.1.1941	4.26.1942	5.21.1942
29	*Edward Rutledge*	3.30.1942	6.21.1942	7.8.1942
30	*Abel Parker Upshur*	4.13.1942	6.28.1942	7.14.1942
31	*William Hawkins*	4.27.1942	7.3.1942	7.20.1942
32	*Thomas Pinckney*	6.22.1942	8.23.1942	9.7.1942
33	*Roger Williams*	6.29.1942	8.30.1942	9.12.1942
34	*John Drayton*	7.4.1942	9.5.1942	9.17.1942
35	*James B. Richardson*	8.23.1942	10.15.1942	10.24.1942
36	*Paul Hamilton*	8.30.1942	10.20.1942	10.29.1942
37	*Henry Middleton*	9.5.1942	10.25.1942	11.4.1942
38	*Collis P. Huntington*	9.17.1942	11.1.1942	11.12.1942
39	*Cornelius Harnett*	9.23.1942	11.6.1942	11.20.1942
40	*Henry Bacon*	9.29.1942	11.11.1942	11.24.1942
41	*Abner Nash*	10.4.1942	11.15.1942	11.27.1942
42	*Joseph Alston*	10.10.1942	11.20.1942	11.30.1942
43	*Paul Hamilton Hayne*	10.15.1942	11.24.1942	12.4.1942
44	*Marshall Elliot*	10.20.1942	11.27.1942	12.9.1942

Sponsor	Type	Disposition
Miss Bernice Pierce	EC2-S-C1 (Liberty)	Scrapped 1966
Miss Shirley A. Staples	EC2-S-C1 (Liberty)	Scrapped 1970
Miss Shirley Lee Robertson	EC2-S-C1 (Liberty Class)	Sold private 1947, scrapped 1968
Miss Harriet May Hancock	EC2-S-C1 (Liberty)	Scrapped 1966
Mrs. C.F. Livingston	EC2-S-C1 (Liberty)	Torpedoed and lost off Sassandra 1943
Mrs. Thomas Hewes	EC2-S-C1 (Liberty)	Scrapped 1968
Miss Rachel Cameron	EC2-S-C1 (Liberty)	Torpedoed and scuttled off Greenland 1942
Miss Jean Maclay	EC2-S-C1 (Liberty)	Blew up in Finschaven 1944, CTL but refloated, scrapped
Miss Anne B. Rutledge	EC2-S-C1 (Liberty)	Scrapped 1961
Mrs. Arthur C. Rohn	EC2-S-C1 (Liberty)	Scrapped 1966
Miss Jean Vendig	EC2-S-C1 (Liberty)	Scrapped 1958
Miss Mary Edith Gregory	EC2-S-C1 (Liberty)	Scrapped 1960
Mrs. William Chanler	EC2-S-C1 (Liberty)	Sold private 1947, sunk 1965
Miss Annie G. Ferguson	EC2-S-C1 (Liberty)	Torpedoed and lost off Durban 1943
Miss Eleanor H. VanValey	EC2-S-C1 (Liberty)	Wrecked 1951 but repaired, scuttled off New Jersey with obsolete ammo 1968
Miss Alberta F. Reissner	EC2-S-C1 (Liberty)	Torpedoed and lost off Algiers 1944
Miss Louise Skinner	EC2-S-C1 (Liberty)	scrapped 1971
Miss Roberta A. Fitzhugh	EC2-S-C1 (Liberty)	scrapped 1968
Miss Ellen C. Hancock	EC2-S-C1 (Liberty)	scrapped 1968
Mrs. William B. McKoy	EC2-S-C1 (Liberty)	Torpedoed and lost in the Barents Sea 1945
Miss J.L. Sprunt	EC2-S-C1 (Liberty)	Scrapped 1964
Miss Mary Craig	EC2-S-C1 (Liberty)	Scrapped 1967
Miss Eva M. Hewett	EC2-S-C1 (Liberty)	Sold private 1947, scrapped 1967
Mrs. John S. Griswold	EC2-S-C1 (Liberty)	Scrapped 1968

APPENDIX I

Hull #	Name of Vessel	Keel Laid	Launch Date	Delivery Date
45	*James Iredell*	9.29.1942	11.29.1942	12.12.1942
46	*Penelope Barker*	10.28.1942	12.1.1942	12.15.1942
47	*Alexander Lillington*	11.1.1942	12.6.1942	12.20.1942
48	*Richard Caswell*	11.6.1942	12.10.1942	12.22.1942
49	*Pocahontas*	11.11.1942	12.13.1942	12.27.1942
50	*Christopher Gadsden*	11.15.1942	12.18.1942	12.31.1942
51	*Betty Zane*	11.20.1942	12.22.1942	12.31.1942
52	*James J. Pettigrew*	11.24.1942	12.24.1942	1.7.1943
53	*Daniel H. Hill*	11.27.1942	12.27.1942	1.10.1943
54	*George Davis*	11.29.1942	12.30.1942	1.13.1943
55	*Walter Raleigh*	12.1.1942	1.5.1943	1.16.1943
56	*John Harvey*	12.6.1942	1.9.1943	1.19.1943
57	*Robert Howe*	12.10.1942	1.13.1943	1.23.1943
58	*Nathaniel Macon*	12.13.1942	1.17.1943	1.26.1943
59	*John Wright Stanly*	12.18.1942	1.19.1943	1.29.1943
60	*Francis Nash*	12.22.1942	1.21.1943	1.31.1943
61	*Ephraim Brevard*	12.24.1942	1.24.1943	2.3.1943
62	*George E. Badger*	12.27.1942	1.26.1943	2.6.1943
63	*Flora MacDonald*	12.30.1942	1.30.1943	2.7.1943
64	*James Sprunt*	1.5.1943	2.3.1943	2.11.1943
65	*Matt W. Ransom*	1.9.1943	2.6.1943	2.16.1943
66	*Furnfold M. Simmons*	1.13.1943	2.10.1943	2.18.1943

Sponsor	Type	Disposition
Miss Helen MacMillan	EC2-S-C1 (Liberty)	Damaged in convoy 1943, repaired, bombed in Naples 1943, repaired, sunk as breakwater off Normandy and abandoned 1944
Miss Anna Wood	EC2-S-C1 (Liberty)	Torpedoed and lost in the Barents Sea 1944
Miss Helen Lovering	EC2-S-C1 (Liberty)	Scrapped 1961
Miss Anne Midyette	EC2-S-C1 (Liberty)	Torpedoed and lost off Paranagua 1943
Miss Mary G. Lett	EC2-S-C1 (Liberty)	Scrapped 1960
Miss Florrie Harrington	EC2-S-C1 (Liberty)	Scrapped 1970
Mrs. G.E. Anderson	EC2-S-C1 (Liberty)	Sold private1947, scrapped 1968
Miss Mildred F. Chapman	EC2-S-C1 (Liberty)	Scrapped 1960
Miss Shirley Jean Beasley	EC2-S-C1 (Liberty)	Scrapped 1964
Mrs. M.F.H. Gouverneur	EC2-S-C1 (Liberty)	Scrapped 1960
Miss Barbara Thompson	EC2-S-C1 (Liberty)	Scrapped 1967
Miss Margaret Groover	EC2-S-C1 (Liberty)	Bombed in Bari 1943, scrapped 1948
Miss Dorothy Matteson	EC2-S-C1 (Liberty)	Scrapped 1971
Miss Mary Frances Miller	EC2-S-C1 (Liberty)	Sold private, 1947, wrecked 1952, CTL but repaired, scrapped 1969
Miss Anne Carter Langston	EC2-S-C1 (Liberty)	Sold private 1947, scrapped 1969
Miss Ann G. Adams	EC2-S-C1 (Liberty)	Sold private 1947, scrapped 1971
Mrs. R.L. Harris	EC2-S-C1 (Liberty)	Scrapped 1972
Mrs. Don M. Hyatt	EC2-S-C1 (Liberty)	Scrapped 1972
Miss Sue H. MacPherson	EC2-S-C1 (Liberty)	Torpedoed and lost off Sierra Leone 1943
Miss Charlotte Sprunt	EC2-S-C1 (Liberty)	Torpedoed and lost off Cuba 1943
Mrs. J.K. Fenimore	EC2-S-C1 (Liberty)	Torpedoed off Casablanca, repaired, sunk as breakwater off Normandy and abandoned 1944
Miss Ella Meadows	EC2-S-C1 (Liberty)	Sold private 1947, scrapped 1968

APPENDIX I

Hull #	Name of Vessel	Keel Laid	Launch Date	Delivery Date
67	*Edward B. Dudley*	1.17.1943	2.13.1943	2.21.1943
68	*Willie Jones*	1.19.1943	2.16.1943	2.24.1943
69	*James Moore*	1.21.1943	2.19.1943	2.27.1943
70	*Alfred Moore*	1.24.1943	2.22.1943	3.2.1943
71	*Woodrow Wilson*	1.26.1943	2.25.1943	3.6.1943
72	*William D. Pender*	1.30.1943	2.28.1943	3.9.1943
73	*William D. Mosley*	2.3.1943	3.5.1943	3.12.1943
74	*Davis L. Swain*	2.6.1943	3.9.1943	3.16.1943
75	*Jonathan Worth*	2.11.1943	3.12.1943	3.19.1943
76	*Matthew T. Goldsboro*	2.13.1943	3.15.1943	3.22.1943
77	*Elisha Mitchell*	2.16.1943	3.18.1943	3.25.1943
78	*Christopher Gale*	2.19.1943	3.21.1943	3.28.1943
79	*William L. Davidson*	2.22.1943	3.24.1943	3.31.1943
80	*Walker Taylor*	2.25.1943	3.28.1943	4.5.1943
81	*Roger Moore*	2.28.1943	3.31.1943	4.8.1943
82	*Robert Rowan*	3.5.1943	4.6.1943	4.13.1943
83	*Thomas W. Bickett*	3.9.1943	4.9.1943	4.15.1943
84	*Horace Williams*	3.12.1943	4.12.1943	4.19.1943
85	*Jose Bonifacio*	3.16.1943	4.14.1943	4.21.1943
86	*Thomas L. Clingman*	3.18.1943	4.17.1943	4.24.1943
87	*David Caldwell*	3.22.1943	4.19.1943	4.26.1943
88	*Waigstill Avery*	3.24.1943	4.22.1943	4.28.1943
89	*Cornelia P. Spencer*	3.29.1943	4.24.1943	4.30.1943
90	*Walter Hines Page*	4.1.1943	4.27.1943	5.4.1943
91	*Storm King*	7.20.1943	9.17.1943	12.3.1943

Sponsor	Type	Disposition
Mrs. L.E. Keith	EC2-S-C1 (Liberty Class)	Torpedoed and lost in the North Atlantic 1943
Mrs. William Fauntleroy	EC2-S-C1 (Liberty)	Sunk as target
Mrs. Charles L. Cornell, Jr.	EC2-S-C1 (Liberty)	Sold private 1947, scrapped 1972
Mrs. James E. McClary	EC2-S-C1 (Liberty)	Scrapped 1961
Mrs. Woodrow Wilson	EC2-S-C1 (Liberty)	Scrapped 1960
Mrs. John Dietrich	EC2-S-C1 (Liberty)	Scrapped 1960
Mrs. Sherwood Dudley	EC2-S-C1 (Liberty)	Scrapped 1962
Mrs. F.A. Kean Jr.	EC2-S-C1 (Liberty)	Sold private 1947, scrapped 1968
Mrs. B.M. Washburn	EC2-S-C1 (Liberty)	Scrapped 1969
Miss Martha Daniels	EC2-S-C1 (Liberty)	Scrapped 1969
Mrs. James T. Monk	EC2-S-C1 (Liberty)	Scrapped 1961
Mrs. H.B. Wynne	EC2-S-C1 (Liberty)	Scrapped 1962
Mrs. Chalmers G. Davidson	EC2-S-C1 (Liberty)	Wrecked 1946, refloated, sold to U.S. Navy, scrapped
Miss Frances G. Taylor	EC2-S-C1 (Liberty)	Scrapped 1959
Miss Alice B. Moore	EC2-S-C1 (Liberty)	Scrapped 1971
Miss Jean A. Huske	EC2-S-C1 (Liberty)	Bombed and lost off Sicily 1943, wreck scrapped 1948
Miss Frances Y. Bickett	EC2-S-C1 (Liberty)	Scrapped 1966
Mrs. F.C. Moore	EC2-S-C1 (Liberty)	Sold private 1947, scrapped 1971
Mrs. Alencastro-Guimaraes	EC2-S-C1 (Liberty Class)	Scrapped 1970
Miss Mary J. Diggs	EC2-S-C1 (Liberty)	Scrapped 1960
Mrs. F.K. Massie	EC2-S-C1 (Liberty)	Wrecked and sunk 1946
Miss Irene Vendig	EC2-S-C1 (Liberty)	Scrapped 1960
Mrs. J.M. Johnson	EC2-S-C1 (Liberty)	Torpedoed and lost in the Indian Ocean 1943
Mrs. Arthur W. Page	EC2-S-C1 (Liberty)	Sold private 1947, reefed off Wachapreague, NC in 1975
Mrs. P.F. Halsey	C2-S-AJ1 (Victory)	To USN 1943 as AP171, sold private 1947, scrapped 1970

APPENDIX I

Hull #	Name of Vessel	Keel Laid	Launch Date	Delivery Date
92	*Cyclone*	7.31.1943	9.27.1943	12.14.1943
93	*Eclipse*	8.3.1943	10.3.1943	12.22.1943
94	*Fleetwing*	8.7.1943	10.8.1943	12.31.1943
95	*Flying Eagle*	8.12.1943	10.12.1943	1.15.1944
96	*Kathay*	8.14.1943	10.19.1943	1.31.1944
97	*Monsoon*	8.20.1943	10.26.1943	2.1.1944
98	*Morning Star*	8.25.1943	11.1.1943	2.22.1944
99	*Northern Light*	9.1.1943	11.9.1943	2.29.1944
100	*White Squall*	9.18.1943	11.16.1943	1.23.1944
101	*Marco Polo*	9.28.1943	11.30.1943	1.28.1944
102	*Midnight*	10.4.1943	12.10.1943	2.7.1944
103	*Starlight*	10.9.1943	12.23.1943	2.15.1944
104	*Napier*	10.13.1943	12.31.1943	2.22.1944
105	*Alden Besse*	10.20.1943	1.11.1944	2.29.1944
106	*Sweepstakes*	10.27.1943	1.22.1944	3.7.1944
107	*Orpheus*	11.2.1943	1.29.1944	3.13.1944
108	*Witch of the Wave*	11.9.1943	2.5.1944	3.16.1944
109	*Noonday*	11.17.1943	2.9.1944	3.26.1944
110	*Talisman*	12.1.1943	2.15.1944	3.31.1944
111	*Sturdy Beggar*	12.10.1943	2.21.1944	4.6.1944
112	*Memnon*	12.23.1943	2.26.1944	4.12.1944
113	*Sea Nymph*	12.31.1943	3.2.1944	4.18.1944
114	*White Falcon*	1.13.1944	3.8.1944	4.24.1944
115	*Fair Wind*	1.24.1944	3.13.1944	4.30.1944
116	*Golden Fleece*	1.31.1944	3.18.1944	5.6.1944

Sponsor	**Type**	**Disposition**
Mrs. T.L. Lanier	C2-S-AJ1 (Victory)	To USN 1944 as *Mount McKinley* (AGC 7), reclassified 1969 as LCC 7, scrapped 1977
Mrs. W.C. Park	C2-S-AJ1 (Victory Class)	To USN 1944 as *Mount Olympus* (AGC 8), scrapped 1973
Mrs. P.A. Wilson	C2-S-AJ1 (Victory)	To USN 1944 as *Wasatch* (AGC 9), scrapped 1960
Mrs. R.B. Slagle	C2-S-AJ1 (Victory)	Sold private 1946, scrapped 1970
Miss Julia Raney	C2-S-AJ1 (Victory)	To USN 1944 as *Auburn* (AGC 10) scrapped 1961
Mrs. P.A. Peeples	C2-S-AJ1 (Victory)	To USN 1944 as *Eldorado* (AGC 11), reclassified 1969 as LCC 11, scrapped 1973
Mrs. R.A. Carter	C2-S-AJ1 (Victory)	To USN 1944 as *Estes* (AGC 12), reclassified 1959 as LCC 12, scrapped 1977
Mrs. J.E. Stewart	C2-S-AJ1 (Victory)	To USN 1944 as *Panamint* (AGC 13), scrapped 1961
Miss Mildred Barnhill	C2-S-AJ1 (Victory)	Sold private 1947, scrapped 1970
Mrs. A.J. Reynolds	C2-S-AJ1 (Victory)	To USN 1944 as *Mount Hood* (AE 11), exploded and lost in the Admiralty Islands 1944
Mrs. K.L. Kellogg	C2-S-AJ1 (Victory)	Sold private 1946, sank 1967
Mrs. M.T. Solomon	C2-S-AJ1 (Victory)	To USN in 1944 as AP 175, sold private 1948, sank 1970
Mrs. C.B. Yearout	C2-S-AJ1 (Victory)	Sold private 1946, scrapped 1968
Miss Justine Besse	C2-S-AJ1 (Victory)	Sold private 1947, scrapped 1969
Mrs. E.W. DeKay	C2-S-AJ1 (Victory)	Sold private 1947, scrapped 1969
Miss Caroline Batson	C2-S-AJ1 (Victory)	Sold private 1947, scrapped 1970
Mrs. C.E. Shimp	C2-S-AJ1 (Victory)	To USN 1944 as *Teton* (AGC 14), scrapped 1962
Mrs. E.K. Bryant	C2-S-AJ1 (Victory)	Sold private 1946, scrapped 1972
Mrs. A.M. McCormick	C2-S-AJ1 (Victory)	Sold private 1946, scrapped 1971
Miss Gertrude Carraway	C2-S-AJ1 (Victory)	Sold private 1946, scrapped 1970
Mrs. H.L. Larsen	C2-S-AJ1 (Victory)	Sold private 1946, scrapped 1972
Mrs. G.E. Via	C2-S-AJ1 (Victory)	Sold private 1947, scrapped 1969
Miss Margaret Sellers	C2-S-AJ1 (Victory)	Sold private 1947, scrapped 1979
Mrs. J.H. Taylor	C2-S-AJ1 (Victory)	Sold private 1947, scrapped 1970
Mrs. H.L. Stevens	C2-S-AJ1 (Victory)	Sold private 1947, scrapped 1968

APPENDIX I

Hull #	Name of Vessel	Keel Laid	Launch Date	Delivery Date
117	*Santa Rita*	2.5.1944	3.25.1944	5.12.1944
118	*Santa Leonor*	2.9.1944	3.31. 1944	5.18.1944
119	*Black Warrior*	2.15.1944	4.8.1944	5.24.1944
120	*Wrangell*	2.21.1944	4.14.1944	5.28.1944
121	*Santa Catalina*	2.26.1944	4.22.1944	6.5.1944
122	*Sirocco*	3.3.1944	4.28.1944	6.11.1944
123	*Santa Elisa*	3.8.1944	5.6.1944	6.17.1944
124	*Winged Racer*	3.13.1944	5.12.1944	6.21.1944
125	*Santa Ines*	3.19.1944	5.20.1944	6.29.1944
126	*Game Cock*	3.25.1944	5.26.1944	7.3.1944
127	*Torrance*	4.1.1944	6.6.1944	6.20.1944
128	*Towner*	4.8.1944	6.13.1944	6.27.1944
129	*Trego*	4.14.1944	6.20.1944	7.4.1944
130	*Tolland*	4.22.1944	6.26.1944	8.13.1944
131	*Trousdale*	4.28.1944	7.3.1944	7.24.1944
132	*Tyrrell*	5.6.1944	7.10.1944	7.30.1944
133	*Shoshone*	5.12.1944	7.17.1944	8.31.1944
134	*Valencia*	5.20.1944	7.22.1944	8.14.1944
135	*Southampton*	5.26.1944	7.28.1944	9.16.1944
136	*Venango*	6.6.1944	8.9.1944	8.25.1944
137	*Starr*	6.13.1944	8.18.1944	9.29.1944
138	*Vinton*	6.20.1944	8.25.1944	9.7.1944
139	*Stokes*	6.26.1944	8.31.1944	10.12.1944
140	*Waukesha*	7.3.1944	9.6.1944	9.20.1944

Sponsor	Type	Disposition
Mrs. Henry Stevenson	C2-S-AJ2 (Victory)	Sold private 1946, scrapped 1968
Mrs. R.H. Patchin	C2-S-AJ1 (Victory)	Sold private 1947, scrapped 1978
Mrs. H.L. Ferguson	C2-S-AJ1 (Victory)	Sold private 1947, scrapped 1971
Mrs. G.T. Cambell	C2-S-AJ1 (Victory)	To USN as *Wrangell* (AE 12), scrapped 1977
Mrs. W.F. Cogswell	C2-S-AJ2(Victory)	Sold private 1946, scrapped 1968
Mrs. C.J. Robinson	C2-S-AJ1 (Victory)	Sold private 1947, scrapped 1971
Mrs. C.C. Mallory	C2-S-AJ2(Victory)	Sold private 1946, scrapped 1969
Mrs. R.M. Hitchins	C2-S-AJ1 (Victory)	To USN 1944 as *Firedrake* (AE 14), scrapped 1977
Mrs. James E. Magner	C2-S-AJ2(Victory)	Sold private 1946, scrapped 1973
Miss Charlene Register	C2-S-AJ1 (Victory)	To USN 1944 as *Vesuvius* (AE 15) scrapped 1974
Miss Marlene DeKay	C2-S-AJ3 (Victory)	To USN 1944 as AKA 76, sold private 1946, scrapped 1972
Mrs. Harold Broudy	C2-S-AJ3 (Victory)	To USN 1944 as AKA 77, sold private 1946, wrecked and sank 1967
Mrs. Marian West Nettles	C2-S-AJ3 (Victory)	To USN 1944 as AKA 78, sold private 1946, scrapped 1969
Miss Beverly Peebles	C2-S-AJ3 (Victory)	To USN 1944 as AKA 64 sold private 1946, scrapped 1971
Mrs. J.R. Craig	C2-S-AJ3 (Victory)	To USN 1944 as AKA 79, sold private 1946, scrapped 1969
Miss Juanita Ogburn	C2-S-AJ3 (Victory)	To USN 1944 as AKA 80, sold private 1946, scrapped 1967
Mrs. N.J. Smith	C2-S-AJ3 (Victory)	To USN 1944 as AKA 65, sold private 1946, scrapped 1971
Mrs. C.L. Merritt	C2-S-AJ3 (Victory)	To USN 1944 as AKA 81, sold private 1946, scrapped 1970
Ens. R.V. Blackwood USNRW	C2-S-AJ3 (Victory)	To USN 1944 as AKA 66, sold private 1946, scrapped 1971
Miss Alana Jane Matthes	C2-S-AJ3 (Victory)	To USN 1944 as AKA 82, sold private 1946, scrapped 1971
Mrs. G.L. Griffin	C2-S-AJ3 (Victory)	To USN 1944 as AKA 67, sold private 1946, scrapped 1970
Mrs. J.W. Kirkpatrick	C2-S-AJ3 (Victory)	To USN 1944 as AKA 83, sold private 1946, scrapped 1971
Mrs. W.D. Woodall	C2-S-AJ3 (Victory)	To USN 1944 as AKA 68, sold private 1946, scrapped 1971
Mrs. H.V. Mason	C2-S-AJ3 (Victory)	To USN 1844 as AKA 84, sold private 1946, scrapped 1970

APPENDIX I

Hull #	Name of Vessel	Keel Laid	Launch Date	Delivery Date
141	*Suffolk*	7.11.1944	9.15.1944	10.23.1944
142	*Wheatland*	7.17.1944	9.21.1944	10.6.1944
143	*Tate*	7.22.1944	9.26.1944	11.3.1944
144	*Woodford*	7.29.1944	10.5.1944	10.19.1944
145	*Todd*	8.10.1944	10.10.1944	11.14.1944
146	*Duplin*	8.18.1944	10.17.1944	10.30.1944
147	*Caswell*	8.25.1944	10.24.1944	11.27.1944
148	*New Hanover*	8.31.1944	10.31.1944	12.6.1944
149	*Lenoir*	9.7.1944	11.6.1944	12.14.1944
150	*Alamance*	9.15.1944	11.11.1944	12.22.1944
151	*Joseph A. Brown*	4.7.1943	4.30.1943	5.7.1943
152	*Robert F. Hoke*	4.10.1943	5.4.1943	5.11.1943
153	*Sallie A. Cotton*	4.13.1943	5.7.1943	5.14.1943
154	*John Owen*	4.15.1943	5.10.1943	5.16.1943
155	*Philip Doddridge*	4.18.1943	5.13.1943	5.19.1943
156	*John Grier Hibben*	4.20.1943	5.15.1943	5.21.1943
157	*Kemp P. Battle*	4.23.1943	5.18.1943	5.24.1943
158	*Robert D. Owen*	4.26.1943	5.21.1943	5.27.1943
159	*John P. Mitchell*	4.28.1943	5.23.1943	5.29.1943
160	*Charles D. McIver*	5.1.1943	5.25.1943	5.31.1943
161	*John M. Morehead*	5.5.1943	5.29.1943	6.4.1943
162	*Hannis Taylor*	5.8.1943	5.31.1943	6.6.1943
163	*Edward Richardson*	5.11.1943	6.4.1943	6.10.1943

Sponsor	Type	Disposition
Mrs. W.T. Dixon	C2-S-AJ3 (Victory)	To USN 1944 as AKA 69, sold private 1946, scrapped 1971
Miss Shirley B. Anderson	C2-S-AJ3 (Victory)	To USN 1944 as AKA 85, sold private 1946, scrapped 1973
Mrs. C.E. Fox	C2-S-AJ3 (Victory Class)	To USN 1944 as AKA 70, sold private 1946, scrapped 1970
Mrs. J.F. McInnis	C2-S-AJ3 (Victory)	To USN 1944 as AKA 86, sold private 1946, scrapped 1973
Mrs. R. Gregg Cherry	C2-S-AJ3 (Victory)	To USN 1944 as AKA 71, sold private 1946, scrapped 1972
Miss Mary Jennette	C2-S-AJ3 (Victory)	To USN 1944 as AKA 87, sold private 1946, scrapped 1971
Mrs. W.H. Williamson	C2-S-AJ3 (Victory)	To USN 1944 as AKA 72, sold private 1946, scrapped 1974
Mrs. O.M. Creekmore Jr.	C2-S-AJ3 (Victory)	To USN 1944 as AKA 73, sold private 1946, scrapped 1970
Mrs. John H. Kerr	C2-S-AJ3 (Victory)	To USN 1944 as AKA 74, sold private 1946, scrapped 1971
Mrs. Carl T. Durham	C2-S-AJ3 (Victory)	To USN 1944 as AKA 75, sold private 1946, scrapped 1971
Mrs. E.K. Proctor	EC2-S-C1 (Liberty)	Scrapped 1975
Mrs. Arthur R. Newcombe	EC2-S-C1 (Liberty)	Torpedoed in the Arabian Sea 1943, refloated and repaired, RN training ship in Bombay 1945, scrapped 1949
Mrs. James Hale Jr.	EC2-S-C1 (Liberty)	Sold private 1947, scrapped 1967
Mrs. R.L. Burnett	EC2-S-C1 (Liberty)	Scrapped 1964
Mrs. A.G. Harvey	EC2-S-C1 (Liberty)	Sold private 1947, scrapped 1969
Mrs. Robert M. Scoon	EC2-S-C1 (Liberty)	Sold private 1947, scrapped 1967
Mrs. G.L. Kennell	EC2-S-C1 (Liberty)	Sold private 1947, scrapped 1968
Mrs. C.B. Davis Jr.	EC2-S-C1 (Liberty)	Sold private 1947, mined off Rijeka and sunk, 1947
Miss Dorothy Sutherland	EC2-S-C1 (Liberty)	Scrapped 1971
Mrs. Harold Miller	EC2-S-C1 (Liberty)	Mined and lost off Belgium 1945
Mrs. John M Morehead	EC2-S-C1 (Liberty)	Sold private 1947, scrapped 1966
Miss Mary Hannis Whitted	EC2-S-C1 (Liberty)	Scrapped 1966
Mrs. K.G. Paxton	EC2-S-C1 (Liberty)	To USN as YAG 1955, scrapped 1972

APPENDIX I

Hull #	Name of Vessel	Keel Laid	Launch Date	Delivery Date
164	*William T. Barry*	5.14.1943	6.8.1943	6.14.1943
165	*Lee S. Overman*	5.16.1943	6.11.1943	6.17.1943
166	*Thomas J. Jarvis*	5.19.1943	6.14.1943	6.20.1943
167	*Joseph LeConte*	5.22.1943	6.17.1943	6.23.1943
168	*Arthur Dobbs*	5.24.1943	6.20.1943	6.27.1943
169	*John Lawson*	5.26.1943	6.24.1943	6.30.1943
170	*Hilary A. Herbert*	5.30.1943	6.27.1943	7.3.1943
171	*Hutchinson I. Cone*	5.31.1943	6.30.1943	7.7.1943
172	*Lawrence D. Tyson*	6.5.1943	7.3.1943	7.10.1943
173	*David F. Houston*	6.9.1943	7.8.1943	7.15.1943
174	*John Merrick*	6.12.1943	7.11.1943	7.18.1943
175	*Charles A. Dana*	6.15.1943	7.15.1943	7.22.1943
176	*Richard P. Hobson*	6.18.1943	7.21.1943	7.28.1943
177	*Clement Clay*	6.21.1943	7.24.1943	7.31.1943
178	*Thomas W. Owen*	6.25.1943	7.17.1943	7.23.1943
179	*Chatham C. Lyon*	6.27.1943	7.27.1943	8.3.1943
180	*James I. McKay*	7.1.1943	7.30.1943	8.6.1943
181	*John N. Maffitt*	7.4.1943	8.4.1943	8.11.1943
182	*George Durant*	7.9.1943	8.7.1943	8.14.1943
183	*Augustus S. Merrimon*	7.12.1943	8.11.1943	8.18.1943
184	*Montford Stokes*	7.16.1943	8.14.1943	8.21.1943
185	*Thomas Pollock*	7.22.1943	8.18.1943	8.25.1943
186	*John Branch*	7.25.1943	8.21.1943	8.28.1943
187	*Skagit*	9.21.1944	11.18.1944	11.28.1944
188	*Union*	9.27.1944	11.23.1943	12.4.1944

Sponsor	Type	Disposition
Mrs. John M. Waterman	EC2-S-C1 (Liberty)	Reefed off Alabama 1975
Miss Margaret A. Gregory	EC2-S-C1 (Liberty)	Mined and lost off Le Havre 1944
Mrs. A.L. Godley	EC2-S-C1 (Liberty)	Scrapped 1961
Mrs. J.E. Rollins	EC2-S-C1 (Liberty)	Sold private 1947, scrapped 1971
Mrs. Cecil H. Bartley	EC2-S-C1 (Liberty)	Sold private 1947, scrapped 1968
Mrs. V.T. Ellis	EC2-S-C1 (Liberty)	Sold private 1947, converted to LNG carrier *Beauvais*, scrapped 1967
Mrs. O.L. Souder	EC2-S-C1 (Liberty)	Sold private 1947, wrecked 1947, CTL but repaired, scrapped 1967
Mrs. J.C. Metzel	EC2-S-C1 (Liberty)	Scrapped 1962
Mrs. Kenneth Gilpin	EC2-S-C1 (Liberty)	Scrapped 1971
Mrs. Robert C. Patton	EC2-S-C1 (Liberty)	Scrapped 1969
Mrs. Martha Merrick Donnel	EC2-S-C1 (Liberty Class)	Scrapped 1967
Miss Frances May	EC2-S-C1 (Liberty)	Reefed off Aransas Pass, TX in 1976
Mrs. Kennedy E. Neill	EC2-S-C1 (Liberty)	Scrapped 1962
Mrs. O.R. Naumann	EC2-S-C1 (Liberty)	Scrapped 1964
Miss Lynne N. Drexler	EC2-S-C1 (Liberty)	Sold private 1947, wrecked and sunk 1963
Mrs. Mattie Clark	EC2-S-C1 (Liberty)	Scrapped 1967
Miss Mary W. Cromartie	EC2-S-C1 (Liberty)	Sold private 1947, scrapped 1967
Miss Florence Pierson	EC2-S-C1 (Liberty)	Scrapped 1966
Miss Eleanor G. James	EC2-S-C1 (Liberty)	Scrapped 1961
Miss Margaret Cuninggim	EC2-S-C1 (Liberty)	Scrapped 1957
Mrs. John Ward Jr.	EC2-S-C1 (Liberty)	Sold private 1947, scrapped 1962
Mrs. N.J. Hines Jr.	EC2-S-C1 (Liberty)	Sold private 1947, sunk 1956
Miss Mary Ann Milburn	EC2-S-C1 (Liberty)	Sold private 1947, wrecked 1961, CTL but refloated, scrapped 1962
Miss Heloise Pike	C2-S-AJ3 (Victory)	To USN 1945 as AKA 105, reclassified 1969 as LKA 105, scrapped 1974
Mrs. W.O. Burgin	C2-S-AJ3 (Victory)	To USN 1945 as AKA 106, reclassified 1969 as LKA 106, scrapped 1977

APPENDIX I

Hull #	Name of Vessel	Keel Laid	Launch Date	Delivery Date
189	*Ottawa*	10.5.1944	11.29.1943	1.5.1945
190	*Prentiss*	10.10.1944	12.6.1944	1.12.1945
191	*Vermilion*	10.17.1944	12.12.1944	12.23.1944
192	*Washburn*	10.24.1944	12.18.1944	12.30.1944
193	*Rankin*	10.31.1944	12.22.1944	1.26.1945
194	*Seminole*	11.7.1944	12.28.1944	2.6.1945
195	*Mount Katmai*	11.11.1944	1.6.1945	2.12.1945
196	*Adirondack*	11.18.1944	1.13.1945	2.4.1945
197	*Great Sitkin*	11.23.1944	1.20.1945	2.19.1945
198	*Pocono*	11.30.1944	1.25.1945	2.15.1945
199	*Paricutin*	12.7.1944	1.30.1945	3.4.1945
200	*Diamond Head*	12.12.1944	2.3.1945	3.11.1945
201	*Taconic*	12.19.1944	2.10.1945	3.6.1945
202	*Stella Lykes*	12.23.1944	2.17.1945	3.21.1945
203	*Ruth Lykes*	12.28.1944	2.24.1945	3.27.1945
204	*American Ranger*	1.7.1945	3.3.1945	4.5.1945
205	*American Banker*	1.14.1945	3.10.1945	4.12.1945
206	*American Farmer*	1.21.1945	3.17.1945	4.19.1945

Sponsor	Type	Disposition
Mrs. W.S. Pritchard	C2-S-AJ3 (Victory)	To USN 1945 as AKA 101, sold private 1947, wrecked and scrapped 1951
Mrs. Roger Williams	C2-S-AJ3 (Victory)	To USN 1945 as AKA 102, sold private 1947, scrapped 1970
Mrs. Rex Freeman	C2-S-AJ3 (Victory)	To USN 1945 as AKA 107, reclassified 1969 as LKA 107, to NDRF 1988
Maj. K.A. Towle, USMCR	C2-S-AJ3 (Victory)	To USN 1945 as AKA 108, reclassified 1969 as LKA 108, scrapped 1980
Mrs. L.C. Freeman	C2-S-AJ3 (Victory)	To USN 1945 as AKA 103, reclassified 1969 as LKA 103, to NDRF 1988, sunk as reef off Florida
Miss Pamela Cole	C2-S-AJ3 (Victory)	To USN 1945 as AKA 104, reclassified 1969 as LKA 104, scrapped 1976
Mrs. A.E. DeMaray	C2-S-AJ1 (Victory)	To USN 1945 as AE 16, scrapped 1974
Mrs. E.L. White	C2-S-AJ1 (Victory)	To USN 1945 as AGC 15, scrapped 1972
Miss Anne Lillian Diamond	C2-S-AJ1 (Victory)	To USN 1945 as AE 17, scrapped 1974
Miss Mary Virginia Carmines	C2-S-AJ1 (Victory)	To USN 1945 as AGC 16, reclassified 1969 as LCC 16, scrapped 1976
Sra. Arias De Garcia Jurado	C2-S-AJ1 (Victory)	To USN 1945 as AE 18, scrapped 1973
Mrs. David Bill	C2-S-AJ1 (Victory)	To USN 1945 as AE 19, sold private 1974, scrapped
Mrs. O.W. Turner	C2-S-AJ1 (Victory)	To USN 1945 as AGC 17, reclassified 1969 as LCC 17, scrapped 1976
Mrs. W.H. Blakeman	C2-S-AJ1 (Victory)	Sold private 1945, scrapped 1971
Mrs. Albert Chandler	C2-S-AJ1 (Victory)	Sold private 1945, scrapped 1971
Mrs. Edmund F. Heard	C2-S-AJ1 (Victory)	Sold private 1963, scrapped 1971
Mrs. Geo. Seidler	C2-S-AJ1 (Victory)	Sold private 1963, scrapped 1971
Mrs. J.B. Woodward Jr.	C2-S-AJ1 (Victory)	Sold private 1964, scrapped 1969

APPENDIX I

Hull #	Name of Vessel	Keel Laid	Launch Date	Delivery Date
207	*Kenneth McKay*	1.26.1945	3.24.1945	4.26.1945
208	*Velma Lykes*	1.31.1945	3.31.1945	5.3.1945
209	*Louise Lykes*	1.31.1945	4.6.1945	5.10.1945
210	*Elizabeth Lykes*	2.12.1945	4.14.1945	5.17.1945
211	*Reuben Tipton*	2.19.1945	4.20.1945	5.24.1945
212	*Harry Culbreath*	2.26.1945	4.26.1945	5.30.1945
213	*Red Gauntlet*	3.5.1945	5.5.1945	6.8.1945
214	*Simoon*	3.10.1945	5.14.1945	6.16.1945
215	*Canvasback*	3.19.1945	5.23.1945	6.23.1945
216	*Tyson Lykes*	3.24.1945	5.30.1945	6.30.1945
217	*Eugene Lykes*	4.2.1945	6.8.1945	7.9.1945
218	*Sue Lykes*	4.7.1945	6.15.1945	7.17.1945
219	*Rattler*	4.16.1945	6.23.1945	7.27.1945
220	*Stag Hound*	4.21.1945	7.2.1945	8.4.1945
221	*Red Jacket*	4.30.1945	7.11.1945	8.11.1945
222	*Resolute*	5.7.1945	7.21.1945	8.22.1945
223	*Courser*	5.15.1945	7.27.1945	8.29.1945
224	*Onward*	5.23.1945	8.4.1945	9.10.1945
225	*Charles Lykes*	5.31.1945	8.11.1945	9.22.1945
226	*Dick Lykes*	6.9.1945	8.20.1945	10.2.1945
227	*Kendall Fish*	6.16.1945	8.27.1945	10.18.1945
228	*Rapid*	6.23.1945	9.12.1945	10.29.1945
229	*Defender*	7.3.1945	9.25.1945	11.9.1945
230	*Whistler*	7.12.1945	10.6.1945	11.23.1945
231	*American Merchant*	7.22.1945	10.19.1945	12.5.1945
232	*American Shipper*	7.28.1945	11.2.1945	12.17.1945
233	*American Forwarder*	8.6.1945	11.10.1945	1.2.1946
234	*American Importer*	8.13.1945	11.23.1945	1.10.1946
235	*American Clipper*	8.21.1945	12.6.1945	1.22.1946
236	*American Scout*	8.28.1945	12.18.1945	2.1.1946
237	*American Traveler*	9.13.1945	1.3.1946	

Sponsor	Type	Disposition
Mrs. J.D. Peters	C2-S-AJ1 (Victory)	Sold private 1945, scrapped 1971
Miss Sandra Ingalls	C2-S-AJ1 (Victory)	Sold private 1945, scrapped 1971
Mrs. Anne P. Myers	C2-S-AJ1 (Victory)	Sold private 1945, scrapped 1972
Mrs. Charles O. Andrews	C2-S-AJ1 (Victory)	Sold private 1945, scrapped 1972
Miss Alice Farrell	C2-S-AJ1 (Victory)	Sold private 1945, scrapped 1971
Miss Mildred Culbreath	C2-S-AJ1 (Victory)	Sold private 1945, scrapped 1971
Mrs. Frederic Smith	C2-S-AJ1 (Victory)	Sold private 1945, scrapped 1971
Miss Miriam Inez Cook	C2-S-AJ1 (Victory)	Sold private 1945, scrapped 1971
Mrs. George W. Hall	C2-S-AJ1 (Victory)	Sold private 1945, scrapped 1972
Mrs. Wm C. Barfield	C2-S-AJ1 (Victory)	Sold private 1945, scrapped 1972
Mrs. F.E. Lykes	C2-S-AJ1 (Victory)	Sold private 1945, scrapped 1970
Miss Elizabeth Randolph	C2-S-AJ1 (Victory)	Sold private 1945, scrapped 1972
Miss Nancy Cowles Taylor	C2-S-AJ1 (Victory)	Sold private 1945, scrapped 1971
Miss Laura Franklin	C2-S-AJ1 (Victory)	Sold private 1945, scrapped 1971
Miss Helen Ravenel	C2-S-AJ1 (Victory)	Sold private 1945, scrapped 1971
Mrs. J.E. Goodwin	C2-S-AJ1 (Victory)	Sold private 1945, scrapped 1971
Miss Elaine Layden	C2-S-AJ1 (Victory)	Sold private 1945, scrapped 1971
Mrs. E.L. Goodson	C2-S-AJ1 (Victory)	Sold private 1945, scrapped 1972
Mrs. T.M. Lykes	C2-S-AJ1 (Victory)	Sold private 1945, scrapped 1970
Mrs. J.M. Lykes	C2-S-AJ1 (Victory)	Sold private 1945, scrapped 1970
Mrs. Carl P. Fish	C2-S-AJ1 (Victory)	Sold private 1945, scrapped 1970
Mrs. A.J. McCarthy	C2-SJ-A5 (Victory)	Sold private 1945, scrapped 1969
Mrs. N.T. Lawrence	C2-SJ-A5 (Victory)	Sold private 1945, scrapped 1970
Miss Janet Carol Gibbons	C2-SJ-A5 (Victory)	Sold private 1945, scrapped 1975
Mrs. C.J. Sullivan	C2-SJ-A5 (Victory)	Sold private 1945, scrapped 1970
Miss Dorothy Mae Walsh	C2-SJ-A5 (Victory)	Sold private 1945, sank 1974
Miss Gladys M. Jones	C2-SJ-A5 (Victory)	Sold private 1946, scrapped 1972
Miss Margaret C. Bray	C2-SJ-A5 (Victory)	Sold private 1946, scrapped 1972
Miss Elizabeth B. Topping	C2-SJ-A5 (Victory)	Sold private 1946, scrapped 1972
Mrs. R.M. Hicks	C2-SJ-A5 (Victory)	Sold private 1946, scrapped 1973
Miss Claire Nevins	C2-SJ-A5 (Victory)	Sold private 1946, scrapped 1972

APPENDIX I

Hull #	Name of Vessel	Keel Laid	Launch Date	Delivery Date
238	*Santa Barbara*	9.28.1945	1.24.1946	
239	*Santa Cecilia*	10.8.1945	2.8.1946	
240	*Santa Margarita*	10.20.1945	3.1.1946	
241	*Santa Maria*	11.3.1945	3.15.1946	
242	*Santa Luisa*	11.12.1945	4.2.1946	
243	*Santa Isabel*	11.27.1945	4.16.1946	

Sponsor	Type	Disposition
Mrs. Alan Corey	C2-SJ-A4 (Victory)	Sold private 1946, scrapped 1969
Mrs. Frederick Byers	C2-SJ-A4 (Victory)	Sold private 1946, scrapped 1970
Miss Helen M. McGann	C2-SJ-A4 (Victory)	Sold private 1946, scrapped 1968
Mrs. Arthur C. Diehl	C2-SJ-A4 (Victory)	Sold private 1946, scrapped 1970
Miss Mary A. Fleming	C2-SJ-A4 (Victory)	Sold private 1946, scrapped 1970
Mrs. Edgar Eyre	C2-SJ-A4 (Victory)	Sold private 1946, scrapped 1970

Appendix II
North Carolina Shipbuilding Co. Officers and Directors

OFFICERS AND DIRECTORS

Homer L. Ferguson, Chairman of the Board, Director
Roger Williams, President, Director
P. F. Halsey, Vice-President and General Manager, Director
John B. Woodward Jr., Director
William E. Blewett Jr., Director
Edmund F. Heard, Director
Robert I. Fletcher, Director
Edward J. Robeson Jr., Director
J. Laurence Sprunt, Director

OFFICERS

Paul A. Wilson, Secretary and Assistant Treasurer
Storer P. Ware, Secretary (resigned 7-31-44)
W. Graham Scott, Treasurer
Thomas L. Lanier, Assistant Comptroller
W.S. McMahon, Assistant Secretary
Kemper L. Kellogg, Assistant Secretary
J. M. Waterman, Assistant Comptroller
F.A. Matthes Jr., Assistant Treasurer

SUPERINTENDENTS AND DIVISION HEADS

W.C. Park, Production Superintendent
J.A. Maclay, Superintendent Hull Construction
E.S. Baysden, Superintendent Hull Outfitting and Machinery
H.K. Peebles, Purchasing Agent
L.K. Hoxton, Assistant Purchasing Agent
J.W. Kirkpatrick, Personnel Director
R.L. Burnett, Assistant Personnel Director
W.F. LaPorte, Plant Engineer

APPENDIX II

DEPARTMENTAL FOREMEN FOR HULL CONSTRUCTION

C.H. Bartley, Anglesmiths
E.O. Beasley, Welding
D.M, Hyatt, Drillers
P.B. Hancock, Shipwrights
F.A. Kean, Fitters
L.E. Keith, Erectors
J.E. McClary, Shipwrights
J.T. Monk, Ship Shed & Anglesmiths
O.R. Naumann, Riveters
H.B. Wynne, Mold Loft

DEPARTMENTAL FOREMEN FOR HULL OUTFITTING AND MACHINERY

C.L. Cornell, Jr., Electricians
J.K. Fenimore, Steam Engineers
R.J. Gregory, Steam Engineers
F.K. Massie, Machine Shop
K.E. Neill, Painters
W.H. Osborne, Joiners
J.T. Pierce, Sheet Metal
D.W. Rivenbank, Yard Riggers
W.J. Robertson, Ship Carpenters
O.L. Souder, Pipe Coverers
O.C. Staples, Plumbers and Pipe Shop
W.D. Woodall, Boiler and Blacksmith

FOREMEN AND DEPARTMENTAL HEADS

John Dietrich, Chief Piece Work Counter
W.M. Fauntleroy, Plant Engineers
A.L. Godley, Chief Hull Engineer
J.M. Johnson, Chief Timekeeper
G.L. Kennell, Chief, Police and Fire Department
R.C. Oxford, Chief Welding Instructor
G.G. Poletika, Chief Machinery Engineer
F.K. Reissner, Transportation
George Hall, Transportation
F.C. Moore, Warehouse
W.K. Sanderson, Steel Storage and Lumber Yard
George E. Via, Chief, Time Study
W.C. Barfield, Chief Accountant
C.E. Enfield, Employment Manager
J.B. Harris, Tabulating Supervisor
C. B. Maynard, Hull Construction Staff Supervisor

P.A. Peebles, Welfare Manager
C.B. Yearout, Safety Engineer
Dr. J.W. Hooper, Medical Director and Chief Surgeon
Dr. D.B. Koonce, Assistant Chief Surgeon

ROLL OF HONOR

During World War II approximately 6,813 men and women left the North Carolina shipbuilding Company to serve in the Armed Forces and Merchant Marine. Thirty-three are known to have died serving their country.

PFC Douglas F. Potter, Wilmington
Frank L. Johnson, Jr., Wilmington
Sgt. Lloyd E, Dale, Watha
PFC William H. Mayers, Acme
Lt. William F. Pritchard, Wilmington
S 2/c Owen C. Fillyaw, Wilmington
Pvt. Kenneth Tant, Middlesex
S 2/c Thomas C. Clarke, Wilmington
Lt. Harold L. Patterson, Kannapolis
PFC Norwood O. Brooks, Wilmington
PFC Malcolm D. Riley, Efland
Pvt. Samuel G. Hatch, Wilmington
S 1/c Ellon E. Davenport, Dover
Sgt. Amos Dobson, Jr., Lynchburg, Va.
Pvt. Alfred L. Baldwin, Wilmington
PFC Arthur W. Jackson, Wilmington
Lynwood A. Corbett, Atkinson
Lt. Robert V. Mercer, Bladenboro
Lt. Bruce C. Robbins, Bostic
Sgt. H.S. Harrelson, Cerro Gordo
MOMM 1/c Edwim H. Avant, Whiteville
Lt. Charles B. Boyd, Wilmington
Pvt. Henry T. Pound, Gaston, S.C.
Pvt. James C. Hudson, Tryon
Sgt. Forest Wadsworth, Clarkton
PFC Ray C. Worley, Barnard
PFC Herman E. Tyson, Wilmington
Cpl. Jack G. Pardy, Madison, S.D.
Paul T. Pittman, Rocky Mount
PFC Edward F. Cline, Wilmington
Cpl. John W. Perry, Raleigh
Capt. A.P. (Byng) Farrar, Chapel Hill
Pvt. Jesse N. Loren, Augusta, Ga.

Appendix III

Alien Passengers Traveling on the USS *Vance*

List or manifest of alien passengers traveling on the USS *Vance* under U.S. Army escort having secret military orders of the U.S. War Department arriving in New York February 25, 1947.

LIST 1

Foltes, Hans	46	Technician
Gengelback, Lesel	32	Housewife
Gengelback, Helga	6	Child
Gengelback, Heike	4	Child
Gothert, Hertha	33	Housewife
Gothert, Hella	10	Student
Gothert, Winfried	8	Student
Gothert, Wolhart	8	Student
Gothert, Reinhart	2	Child
Hartund, Friedrich	26	Engineer
Heinrich, Luise	22	Housewife
Heinrich, Hildegard	11	Student
Heinrich, Eva	5	Child

Heinrich, Klaus	2	Child
Hoffmann, Frederich	36	Chemist
Jacobi, Kathe	29	Housewife
Kandziora, Renate	12	Student
Keil, Alfred	33	Physicist
Knacka, Margrete	32	Housewife
Knacka, Rudiger	5	Child
Knacka, Brigitte	3	Child
Kostlin, Louise	74	Dependent
Kulikow, Antoli	62	Dependent
Lange, Nadeschda	37	Housewife
Lange, Klara	13	Student
Lange, Peter	6	Child
Lange, Elisabeth	3	Child
Meyer, Hermann	48	Chemist
Mueller, Bozina	35	Housewife
Mueller, Gabrielle	3	Child

LIST 2

Ammann, Margarete	49	Housewife
Ammann, Eric	21	Student
Ammann, Brigitte	19	Student
Ammann, Ellen	17	Student

Ammann, Margret	16	Student
Ammann, Hans-Hugo	11	Student
Ammann, Harriet	8	Student
Arnold, Marianne	32	Housewife
Arnold, Ingrid	2	Child
Axster, Ilse	51	Housewife
Axster, Wendelin	21	Student
Axster, Oliver	15	Student
Baseler, Maria	20	Student
Beichel, Hildegarde	22	Housewife
Beichel, Sigrid	2	Child
Beinert, Helmut	33	Chemist
Benz, Emil	33	Technician
Benzinger, Theodor	41	Medicine
Boccius, Edith	35	Housewife
Boccius, Ilse	7	Child
Boccius, Gunter	3	Child
Drawe, Charlotte	32	Housewife
Eckert, Josephine	42	Housewife
Eckert, Christe	11	Child
Eckert, Elke	6	Child
Eckert, Karin	4	Child

Eckert, Dieter	3	Child
Eisenhardt, Anna-Marie	45	Housewife
Eisenhardt, Otto-Frank	13	Student
Eisenhardt, Anneliese	9	Student

LIST 3

Patt, Edith	32	Housewife
Patt, Peter	9	Student
Patt, Jurgen	6	Child
Ramm, Ruth	34	Housewife
Ramm, Uta	6	Child
Ramm, Hartmut	4	Child
Rose, Heinrich	38	Medicine
Schelp, Gertrud	31	Housewife
Schelp, Rainer	2	Child
Schmitt, Lotte	36	Housewife
Schmitt, Rolf	7	Student
Schmitt, Incgelorg	47	Medicine
Schuler, Berta	26	Housewife
Schuler, Klaus	4	Child
Seeler, Henry	41	Engineer
Tessmann, Ilse	33	Housewife

Vogt, Richard	52	Engineer
Von Hoermann, Charlotte	39	Housewife
Von Onain, Hans	35	Physicist
Winkler, Eva	21	Physicist
Weinig, Anna	47	Housewife
Witzky, Gertrud	40	Housewife
Witzky, Hans	12	Student
Witzky, Gertrud	9	Student
Witzky, Lily	2	Child
Wolframm, Max	34	Engineer

Notes

CHAPTER I

1. The Maritime Commission was created at first in 1936 to modernize the American merchant marine. It was to accomplish this task by distributing shipbuilding and ship operating subsidies among builders and operator alike. By the late thirties, the commission had long-range plans for bringing the American merchant marine back on its feet again. Vessels such as the *President* series of liners, the *America* and numerous cargo styles were evidence of the rebirth of shipbuilding and shipping fraternity.

In World War II the shipbuilding industry, mobilized under the Maritime Commission, set records of production which have never been equaled. New shipyards were built and a labor force of over 640,000 persons was employed. Some 55 million tons of vessels were produced during the war years. The commission hoped to build vessels faster than they were being sunk. Speed was of the utmost importance. To this end the commission developed a number of streamlined assembly methods that revolutionized the shipbuilding industry. Records such as these and one at North Carolina Shipbuilding Company were not achieved without attendant crisis and confusion. Under the able leadership of Admiral Emory Scott Land the rough waters were made smooth and commission vessels sailed forth to join the war effort. Land was not one to mince words. He stated that personally he was not in favor of the "commission form" of government. He preferred instead "a one-man show and shoot him at sunrise if he doesn't run it right."

The jobs of selecting the yard sites, recruiting, training and housing the labor force, collective bargaining and overlapping union jurisdiction were solved by the commission, which was subjected at times to pressure applied both by the White House and private shipyard owners.

The mild climate in the South played an important role in the selection of a number of Southern sites by the U.S. Maritime Commission. The commission had found in a number of the early contract plants (which were located primarily in the industrial coastal areas, as far north as Bath, Maine) that inclement weather in the winter months had delayed construction on a number of vessels. As a result of a consistent effort that had been made to locate plant expansion in areas that 1) had not been used before in the maritime war effort (and hence a source of untapped labor) and 2) were located in milder climates. This decision proved beneficial to the economies of the Southern states during the war.

2. Frederic C. Lane, *Ships for Victory* (Baltimore, 1951), 40, 47–49.

3. Ibid., 50.
4. Emory Scott Land to Josiah Bailey, October 8, 1940, Josiah Bailey Papers, Manuscript Department, Perkins Library, Duke University, hereinafter cited as Bailey Papers.
5. Thomas F. Little to the *Charlotte Observer*, November 23, 1939, Bailey Papers.
6. Thomas F. Little to A. Hand James, October 31, 1939, Bailey Papers.
7. Josiah Bailey to Thomas Wright, May 25, 1940, Bailey Papers.
8. James Wade to Wilmington Shipyard Committee, July 9, 1940, North Carolina Department of Conservation and Development Papers, North Carolina State Archives, Raleigh, hereinafter cited as Department of Conservation and Development Papers.
9. Wade to Wilmington Shipyard Committee, July 9, 1940.
10. Wade to Wilmington Shipyard Committee, July 9, 1940.
11. Josiah Bailey to Benjamin Royal, September 20, 1940, Bailey Papers; Bailey to Stanley Woodland, November 22, 1940, Bailey Papers.
12. Josiah Bailey to Admiral Emory Scott Land, October 5, 1940, Bailey Papers; Bailey to Frank Knox, October 5, 1940, Bailey Papers.
13. Louis Moore to Norman Lombard, October 22, 1940, Department of Conservation and Development Papers.
14. *Five Years of North Carolina Shipbuilding*, 8.
15. Ibid.
16. "Wilmington Selected After Exhaustive Study," undated clipping from *Charlotte News*, in North Carolina Shipbuilding Company Scrapbook, private collection of Mr. Adrian Hurst, Wilmington, NC.
17. "Wilmington Selected After Exhaustive Study," Hurst Collection.
18. Lane, *Ships for Victory*, 37.
19. Interview with William S. McMahon, Assistant Secretary of the North Carolina Shipbuilding Company (conducted in Newport News, VA, April–May 1976). "Wilmington Selected After Exhaustive Study," Hurst Collection.
20. Lane, *Ships for Victory*, 35.
21. J. Melville Broughton to James T. Anderson, November 11, 1940, Department of Conservation and Development Papers.

CHAPTER II

22. Emory Scott Land to William S. Knudsen, November 8, 1940, U.S. Maritime Commission Records, Record Group 178, National Archives, Washington, D.C., hereinafter cited as Maritime Commission Records I.
23. Land to Knudsen, November 13, 1940, Maritime Commission Records I.
24. Knudsen to Franklin D. Roosevelt, November 19, 1940, Maritime Commission Records I; Emory Scott Land, *Winning the War with Ships*, 7; "Shipbuilding at Wilmington," *The State*, September 12, 1944, 11; Homer L. Ferguson to Josiah Bailey, March 20, 1941, Bailey Papers.
25. Benjamin F. Royal to Josiah Bailey, November 29, 1940, Bailey Papers; Bailey to Land, December 4, 1940, Bailey Papers; Land to Bailey, December 7, 1940, Bailey Papers; "Brief on Shipyard at Morehead City, N.C.," Bailey Papers.

26. J. Melville Broughton to Harold D. Cooley, December 28, 1940, Governors Papers, J. Melville Broughton, State Archives, Raleigh, hereinafter cited as Broughton Papers; Royal to Graham Barden, December 28, 1940, Bailey Papers; "Brief on Shipyard at Morehead City, N.C.," Bailey Papers.
27. Thomas Little to Broughton, January 8, 1941, Broughton Papers.
28. Little to Broughton, January 8, 1941, Broughton Papers; Homer L. Ferguson to Schuyler O. Bland, January 13, 1941, Bailey Papers; Bailey to Royal, January 15, 1941, Bailey Papers; Roosevelt to Little, January 21, 1941, Bailey papers; Bailey to Royal, January 30, 1941, Bailey Papers; Homer L. Ferguson to Josiah Bailey, March 20, 1941, Bailey Papers.
29. Bailey to Samuel W. Robinson, April 4, 1941, Bailey Papers; Broughton to Royal, August 15, 1941, Broughton Papers; Royal to Little, August 13, 1941, Broughton Papers.
30. Little to William Franklin Knox, September 1, 1941, Broughton Papers; Little to Graham Barden, September 17, 1941, Graham Barden Papers, Manuscript Department, Perkins Library, Duke University, Durham, NC, hereinafter cited as Barden Papers; P.W. Foote to Little, August 29, 1941, Broughton Papers.
31. Bailey to Royal, October 11, 1941, Broughton Papers; Royal to Bailey, October 13, 1941, Bailey Papers; Barden to Bailey, October 13, 1941, Barden Papers; Bailey to Royal, October 15, 1941, Bailey Papers; Broughton to Bailey, November 4, 1941, Broughton Papers; Broughton to Marvin McIntyre, November 6, 1941, Broughton Papers.
32. Little to Josephus Daniel, December 9, 1941, Barden Papers; Bailey to Broughton, January 8, 1942, Broughton Papers; Broughton to Bailey, January 20, 1942, Broughton Papers; Broughton to Land, January 20, 1942, Broughton Papers; Bailey to Broughton, February 23, 1942, Broughton Papers; Broughton to Bailey, February 19, 1942, Broughton Papers.

CHAPTER III

33. *Five Years of North Carolina Shipbuilding*, 8; "Shipbuilding at Wilmington," *The State* September 12, 1944, 10.
34. *Five Years of North Carolina Shipbuilding*, 9; Minutes of the United States Maritime Commission, June 20, 1942, 22312, Record Group 178, U.S. Maritime Commission Records, National Archives, Washington, D.C, hereinafter cited as Maritime Commission Minutes.
35. Ibid. 108–17.
36. Ibid., 108.
37. Ibid., 220–21.
38. Ibid., 218, 222, 227.
39. *Five Years of North Carolina Shipbuilding*, 10.
40. Lane, *Ships for Victory*, 208–09.
41. F.G. Fassett Jr., *The Shipbuilding Business in the United States of America*, I, 213.
42. Fassett, *Shipbuilding Business*, I, 213.

43. The building is shown in an aerial photograph in *Five Years of North Carolina Shipbuilding*, along with an interior photograph of the gear assembly building.
44. *Five Years of North Carolina Shipbuilding*, 11, 24–25.
45. Maritime Commission Minutes, December 22, 1941, 203000.
46. J.W. Steiner, "How to Light a Shipway," *Marine Engineering and Shipping Review* 47 (May 1941), 176.
47. Roy A. Palmer to William S. McMahon, December 8, 1942, Maritime Commission Record I; William S. McMahon to Office of Civilian Defense, Charlotte, N.C., December 10, 1942, Maritime Commission Records I; William S. Pritchard to Horner C. Fisher, December 8, 1942, Maritime Commission Records I, hereinafter cited as Pritchard's Report.
48. Pritchard's Report, 2.
49. Ibid.
50. Ibid.
51. Ibid.
52. Ibid.
53. *The North Carolina Shipbuilder* (January 1, 1943).

CHAPTER IV

54. Federal Writers' Project, *North Carolina: a Guide to the Old North State*, 247–49.
55. U.S. Bureau of Labor Statistics, *A Statistical Summary of the Wilmington Area; New Hanover County, North Carolina* (Washington, D.C., 1943), 1.
56. U.S. Bureau of Labor Statistics, *A Statistical Summary of the Wilmington Area*, 2.
57. Ibid., 2, 9; J. Cargile Johnson, Interview, Newport News, VA, February 23, 1979.
58. U.S. Bureau of Labor Statistics, *A Statistical Summary of the Wilmington Area*, 9, 11.
59. Ibid., 12; Lowell J. Carr, *Willow Run*, 87–120, 137–139.
60. J. Weaver Kirkpatrick to Corrington McGill, November 30, 1943, Records of the Committee for Congested Production Areas, Record Group 212, National Archives, Washington, D.C.; J.F. McInnis to Maritime Commission, October 8, 1942, Maritime Commission Minutes, 23167; *North Carolina Shipbuilder*, October, 1943; "Report of Housing Program," July 15, 1942, Maritime Commission Minutes, 22517.
61. Agnes E. Meyer, *Journey through Chaos*, 222; John Morton Blum, *V was for Victory*, 226–27.
62. Meyer, *Journey through Chaos*, 224.
63. Ibid.; "Feeding Conditions at various yards," June 5, 1943, Maritime Commission Records I; Records of the Committee for Congested Production Areas, Record Group 212, National Archives, Washington, D.C.; *North Carolina Shipbuilder*, April 1943; January 1943; September 1943.
64. *North Carolina Shipbuilder*, June 1943.
65. "Report on transportation conditions in the various yards," February 8, 1943, Maritime Commission Minutes, 23978, 23991; "Report on transportation conditions in the various yards," February 22, 1944, Maritime Commission Minutes, 27609; "Report on the Formyduval lease," February 21, 1947, Maritime Commission Minutes, 33147; McMahon, Interview; Carr, *Willow Run*, 13, 168, 83.

66. Roger Williams to Frederic C. Lane, May 5, 1947, Maritime Commission Records I; Meyer, *Journey Through Chaos*, 225; "Report of Conditions in the various yards—Wilmington," November 4, 1943; Records of the Committee for Congested Production Areas, Record Group 212, National Archives, Washington, D.C.; Spencer B. King Jr. *Selective Service in North Carolina in World War II* (Chapel Hill, N.C., 1949), 164-165.
67. "Demand-Supply supplement for Wilmington," April 15, 1944, War Manpower Commission Records, Record Group 183, National Archives, Washington, D.C.; *Five Years of North Carolina Shipbuilding*, 7, 19; Meyer, *Journey Through Chaos*, 225; "Resurvey of employment situation in Wilmington," August 10, 1942, Office of Community War Service records, Record Group 215, National Archives, Washington, D.C., McMahon, Interview; King, *Selective Service in North Carolina in World War II*, 136–37.
68. Meyer, *Journey through Chaos*, 225; McMahon, Interview; Reaves, *Strength Through Struggle*, 64–67.
69. Katherine Archibald, *Wartime Shipyard* (Berkeley, 1947), 60–61; McMahon, interview.
70. Archibald, *Wartime Shipyard*, 67–69.
71. Ibid., 69.
72. Ibid., 78.
73. Merl E. Reed, "The FEPC, the Black Worker and the Southern Shipyards," in *South Atlantic Quarterly* 74 (Autumn 1975), 447.
74. Reed, "The FEPC, the Black Worker and the Southern Shipyards," 488; Van Gelder to John Brown, April 3, 1935, IUMSWA files, University of Maryland.
75. Reed, "The FEPC, the Black Worker and the Southern Shipyards," 448–59.
76. *North Carolina Shipbuilder*, January 1943.
77. Ibid.
78. Ibid.
79. Ibid.
80. Edna Cantwell to Women's Bureau, September 17, 1943, Maritime Commission Records I.
81. Ibid.
82. Ibid.
83. Mabel M. Grimes to Women's Bureau, September 17, 1943; Leila Rupp, *Mobilizing Women for War*, 145–56.
84. Mabel M. Grimes to Women's Bureau, September 17, 1943; McMahon, interview.
85. Mabel M. Grimes to Women's Bureau, September 17, 1943.
86. U.S. Women's Bureau, *Employing Women in Shipyards* (Washington, D.C., 1944), 1–4; Josephine Von Milkos, *I Took a War Job* (New York, 1943), 19– 23; Ann Pendleton (pseud. of Mary Beatty Trask), *Hit the Rivet, Sister*, 1–17; Virginia Snow Wilkinson, "From Housewife to Shipfitter," *Harper's* 187 (September 1943), 328–37; Augusta H. Clawson, *Shipyard Diary of a Woman Welder*, 1–53; Laura Nelson Baker, *Wanted: Women in War Industry: The Complete Guide to a War Factory Job*, 4–36.
87. The bureau collected data on women's employment and made "recommendations and suggestions for promoting conditions conducive to the most efficient and productive employment of women shipyard workers."

88. U.S. Women's Bureau, *Employing Women in Shipyards*, 6, 7.
89. Mabel M. Grimes to Women's Bureau, September 17, 1943; U.S. Women's Bureau, *Employing Women in Shipyards*, 1; *Five Years of North Carolina Shipbuilding*, 1.
90. *North Carolina Shipbuilder*, February 1943; D.L. Hartnett, "Industrial Safety Survey of the North Carolina Shipbuilding Company," June 7, 1943, 1–15; Maritime Commission Records, Record Group 178, Federal Records Center, Suitland, Maryland, hereinafter cited as Maritime Commission Records II; "Maritime Commission Safety Survey Card File," Maritime Commission Records II; "Fatal Work Injuries in Shipyards: 1943–1944," 1–14; Maritime Commission Records II.
91. D.L. Hartnett, "Industrial Safety Survey of the North Carolina Shipbuilding Company," 1–15.

CHAPTER V

92. Gary M. Fink, *Labor Unions*, 210–11.
93. Ibid.
94. Ibid., 211.
95. Robert L. Burnett, Oral Interview in Wilmington, North Carolina, February 23, 1978, hereinafter cited as Burnett, Interview.
96. "North Carolina Shipbuilding Company vs. Industrial Union of Marine and Shipbuilding Workers of America," 51 NLRB 252; *Shipyard Worker*, October 8, 1945; October 29, 1945; February 18, 1946.
97. *Shipyard Worker*, August 28, 1942.
98. Ibid., September 13, 1942; October 16, 1942; Percy F. Halsey, Oral Interview in Newport News, VA, May 12, 1976, hereinafter cited as Halsey, interview; Burnett, interview.
99. *Shipyard Worker*, October 16, 1942.
100. *Shipyard Worker*, September 25, 1942; M.H. Goldstein to Lyman Colvert, April 2, 1943, IUMSWA files.
101. *Shipyard Worker*, October 23, 1942; Burnett, interview.
102. *Shipyard Worker*, October 30, 1942.
103. Ibid.
104. Ibid., November 6, 1942.
105. *Shipyard Worker*, January 23, 1943; M.H. Goldstein to Lyman Colvert, April 2, 1943, IUMSWA files.
106. *Shipyard Worker*, February 6, 1943.
107. Lyman C. Covert to Harry A. Millis, July 28, 1943, "North Carolina Shipbuilding Company vs. Industrial Union of Marine and Shipbuilding Workers of America," National Labor Relations Board Records, 3-R-1237, Record Group 25, Federal Records Center, Suitland, Maryland, hereinafter cited as NLRB Records, 3-R-1237.
108. *North Carolina Shipbuilding Company vs. Industrial Union of Marine and Shipbuilding Workers of America*, 51 NLRB, 251–56.
109. Ibid., 255.
110. Ibid., 251–56.

111. Ross M. Madden to Oscar S. Smith, April 4, 1944, "North Carolina Shipbuilding Company vs. Industrial Union of Marine and Shipbuilding Workers of America," National Labor Relations Board Records, 5-R-1528, Record Group 25, Federal Records Center, Suitland, Maryland, hereinafter cited as NLRB Records, 5-R-1528.
112. "Objections of Industrial Union of Marine and Shipbuilding Workers of America," September 14, 1943, "North Carolina Shipbuilding Company vs. Industrial Union of Marine and Shipbuilding Workers of America," National Labor Relations Board Records, R-5455, Record Group 25, Federal Records Center, Suitland, Maryland, hereinafter cited as NLRB Records, R-5455.
113. Roger Williams to Gerard Reilly, December 2, 1943, NLRB Records, R-5455.
114. Williams to Reilly, December 2, 1943, NLRB Records, R-5455.
115. *Shipyard Worker*, December 17, 1943; Lyman Covert, "Memorandum on Labor Board Election," September 19, 1943, IUMSWA files.
116. *Shipyard Worker*, December 17, 1943; October 16, 1943; December 24, 1943.
117. Ibid., December 31, 1943.
118. Ibid.
119. Roger Williams to Albert C. Hill, March 9, 1943, Maritime Commission Records I.
120. Halsey, interview; Williams to Hill, March 9, 1943.
121. An independent union controls the Newport News yard, while AFL/CIO still attempts to gain foothold within.
122. "Brief in Support of Motion for Reconsideration," August 4, 1943, NLRB Records, R-5455.
123. *Shipyard Worker*, April 5, 1944.
124. Ross M. Madden to Oscar S. Smith, April 4, 1944, NLRB Records, 5-R-1528.
125. "Decision and Direction of Election," June 29, 1944, NLRB Records, 5-R-1528.
126. *Shipyard Worker*, June 9, 1944; June 10, 1944.
127. Ibid., July 17, 1944.
128. Ross M. Madden to Oscar S. Smith, November 27, 1946, "North Carolina Shipbuilding Company vs. Industrial Union of Marine and Shipbuilding Workers of America," National Labor Relations Board Records, 5-C-1565, Record Group 25, Federal Records Center, Suitland, Maryland, hereinafter cited as NLRB Records, 5-C-1565; Earle K. Shawe to Oscar S. Smith, November 28, 1946, NLRB Records, 5-C-1565.
129. "Order Approving Settlement Stipulation," December 2, 1946, NLRB Records, 5-C-1565. Each day's testimony was numbered into the court record. The record consists of a ninety-six-volume transcript. The complete record is some 18,000 pages long and is one of the largest case files in Record Group 25. The trial examiner John J. Fitzpatrick issued an *Interim Report* of his findings in the 5-C-1565 case on September 10, 1946. It appears that no copy of the *Interim Report* has survived in the NLRB files.
130. *Shipyard Worker*, January 29, 1945; "Transcript of Hearings North Carolina Shipbuilding Company vs. Industrial Union of Marine and Shipbuilding Workers of America," National Labor Relations Board Records, 5-C-1565, Record Group 25, Federal Records Center, Suitland, Maryland, 745, 766, hereinafter cited as "Transcript of Hearings," NLRB Records, 5-C-1565.

131. *Shipyard Worker*, January 29, 1945; "Transcript of Hearings," NLRB Records, 5-C-1565, 745, 766.
132. *Shipyard Worker*, January 29, 1945.
133. Ibid., February 5, 1945.
134. Ibid.
135. Ibid., February 12, 1945.
136. "Transcript of Hearings," NLRB Records, 5-C-1565, 2919-2925.
137. Ibid., 2910-2925.
138. Ibid., 5-C-1565, 2527-2537.
139. Ibid., 5-C-1565, 2547-2548.
140. *Shipyard Worker*, February 12, 1945.
141. Ibid., February 26, 1945.
142. Ibid., March 5, 1945; Lyman Covert, "Memorandum on Labor Board Election," September 14, 1943, IUMSWA files.
143. "Transcript of Hearings,"NLRB Records, 5-C-1565, 6055-6061.
144. *Shipyard Worker*, March 26, 1945.
145. Ibid., July 2, 1945.
146. "Answer of the Respondent," November 6, 1944, NLRB Records, 5-C-1565.
147. "Motion for Extension of Time to File Exceptions," September 39, 1946, NLRB Records, 5-C-1565.
148. Settlement outlined in memo of Earle K. Shawe to Oscar S. Smith, November 26, 1946, NLRB Records, 5-C-1565.
149. William J. Avrutis to Archie Pruitt, September 17, 1946, NLRB Records, 5-C-1565.
150. Earle K. Shawe to Oscar S. Smith, November 26, 1946, NLRB Records, 5-C-1565.
151. Shawe to Smith, November 26, 1946; Earl K. Shawe undated list entitled "Vital Statistics", t.l., 3p., IUMSWA papers; "The Board of Missing Heirs Radio Program" transcript, April 23, 1947, IUMSWA papers; "North Carolina Shipbuilding Company Distribution of Payment of $65,000," dated received April 24, 1947, t.l., 3p. IUMSWA papers; James F. Waters to Elwood Peoples, May 2, 1947, t.l.s., 1p., IUMSWA papers; "Benefactor of Babes", *Time*, April 14, 1941; The Radio Program was sometimes called either the "Board" or "Court" of Missing Heirs.
152. *Shipyard Worker*, February 18, 1946; *North Carolina Shipbuilding Company v. Industrial Union of Marine and Shipbuilding Workers of America, Intermediate Report*, National Labor Relations Board, September 10, 1946, IUMSWA Files.
153. "Transcript of Hearings," NLRB Records, 5-C-1565, 7543-7557; John L. Blackman, "Navy Policy Toward the Labor Relations of its War Contractors, Part One," *Military Affairs*, 18 (Winter 1954), 176–87; John L. Blackman, "Navy Policy Toward the Labor Relations of its War Contractors, Part Two, *Military Affairs*, 19 (Spring 1955) 21–31.

CHAPTER VI

154. *Five Years of North Carolina Shipbuilding*, 10–14.
155. Lane, *Ships for Victory*, 28.
156. Ibid., 28-29.

157. Ibid., 30-31.
158. Ibid., 572.
159. U.S. Navy Secretary. *Final Report of a Board of Investigation to Inquire into the design and methods of construction of welded steel merchant vessels*, 19–85.
160. Lane, *Ships for Victory*, 80.
161. Lane, *Ships for Victory*, 77; John Gorley Bunker, *Liberty Ships: The Ugly Ducklings of World War II* (Annapolis, 1972), 6.
162. Lane, *Ships for Victory*, 84–88.
163. Ibid., 67, 574.
164. Ibid., 579.
165. Ibid., 578, 583.
166. Ibid., 582–83; Bunker, *Liberty Ships*, 105–09, 121–22, 147; Henry C. Meyer, "Some design problems of the Liberty Cargo Ships," *Journal of Engineering Education*, 33 (January 1943) 454–562.
167. *Five Years of North Carolina Shipbuilding*, 10; L.A. Sawyer, *Victory Ships and Tankers*, 8.
168. Bunker, *Liberty Ships*, 175–81.
169. L.A. Sawyer, *The Liberty Ships*, 21–29; *Five Years of North Carolina Shipbuilding*, 14; Alexander Crosby Brown, *The Good Ships of Newport News: An Informal Acccount of Ships, Shipping and Shipbuilding in the Lower Chesapeake Bay*, 83–93.

CHAPTER VII

170. "North Carolina Shipbuilding Company, Wilmington, NC, WWII Construction Record," November 2006, 7. www.coltoncompany.com/shipbldg/ussbldrs/wwii/merchantshipsbuilders/northcarolina.htm.
171. "Medicine—Voyage of the Vance," *Time*, June 3, 1946, 921–22; Emory A. Massman, *Hospital Ships of World War II*, Jefferson, N.C., McFarland & Company, 1999, 197–219; "List or Manifest of Alien Passengers for the United States Immigrant Inspector at Port of Arrival—New York, February 25, 1947," http://www.magazinepublisher.com/family/images/p51-56.
172. "North Carolina Shipbuilding Company, Wilmington, NC, WWII Construction Record," p.5–7; Benedetto, William, *Sailing into the Abyss*, 182–85, 210, 233–34; "SS Badger State," 3pp., December 2006, www.statesmarinelines.com/ships/badger_state.htm; "USS Starlight (AP-175)," 2pp., December 2006, http://www.navsource.org/archives/09/22175.htm.
173. "North Carolina Shipbuilding Company, Wilmington, NC, WWII Construction Record," p.7; "Grace Line - Grace Line Postcards," 18pp., November 2006, www.simplonpc.co.uk/GraceLinePCs.html
174. "USS Pocono (AGC-16)," *Dictionary of American Naval Fighting Ships*, 2, November 2006, www.history.navy.mil/danfs/p5/pocono.htm
175. "USS Pocono (AGC-16)"; "John T's Navy/Seabee Experience—Pocono History," 5pp. November 2005, www.geocities.com/the17seabee/pocono/16hist.html
176. "USS Pocono (AGC-16)"; "John T's Navy/Seabee Experience—Pocono History," 1.
177. "USS Pocono (AGC-16)"; "John T's Navy/Seabee Experience—Pocono History," 1–2.

178. "Spike and the Gator Navy," November 2006, 3, www.usspocono.org/spike.html; "Pocono Sea Stories," November 2006, 3, www.usspocono.org/sea-stories.html; "USS Pocono (AGC-16)"; "John T's Navy/Seabee Experience—Pocono History," 5.
179. "Estes," *Dictionary of American Naval Fighting Ships*, November 2006, www.history.navy.mil/danfs/e5/estes.htm; "AGC/LCC-2 Estes" *NavSource Online: Amphibious Photo Archive*, November 2006, www.navsource.org/archives/10/0112.htm.
180. "Rankin," Dictionary of American Naval Fighting Ships, November 2006, 2, www.history.navy.mil/danfs/r2/rankin.htm; "USS Rankin (AKA-103)—Her History," November 2006, 3, www.rankin.org/id35.htm; "USS Rankin (AKA-103)," *Wikipedia*, November 2006, 5, en.wikipedia.org/wiki/USS_Rankin_(AKA-103).
181. "Rankin"; "USS Rankin (AKA-103)—Her History"; "USS Rankin (AKA-103)."
182. "USS Rankin (AKA-103)."

CHAPTER VIII

183. Maritime Commission Minutes, December 15, 1948, 52253.
184. *Wilmington Star*, November 10, 1945.
185. Ibid.. February 6, 1946.
186. Mr. Halsey was reluctant to speak of his role in the postwar period in an interview.
187. *Wilmington Star*, August 31, 1946.
188. Maritime Commission Minutes, July 11, 1946, 32262.
189. Ibid.
190. R.B. Page to U.S. Maritime Commission, November 24, 2946, Governors Papers, R. Gregg Cherry, North Carolina State Archives, Raleigh, NC, hereinafter cited as Cherry Papers.
191. R.B. Page to U.S. Maritime Commission, November 13, 1946, Cherry Papers.
192. Maritime Commission Minutes, December 15, 1946, 52251; *Wilmington Star*, December 13, 1946.
193. Maritime Commission Minutes, December 15, 1946, 52253.
194. R.B. Page to U.S. Maritime Commission, November 23, 1946, Cherry Papers.
195. *Wilmington Star*, January 31, 1947; *Raleigh News and Observer*, January 31, 1947.
196. *Wilmington Star*, February 27, 1947; *Wilmington Star*, February 28, 1947.
197. W.W. Smith to J. Bayard Clark, March 19, 1947, Cherry Papers.
198. J. Bayard Clark to R. Gregg Cherry, March 31, 1947, Cherry Papers.
199. Maritime Commission Minutes, December 15, 1948, 52253.
200. *Wilmington Star*, March 27, 1947.
201. Ibid., November 27, 1947; McMahon, interview; Burnett, interview.
202. *Wilmington Star*, May 7, 1948; McMahon, interview.
203. *Wilmington Star*, November 17, 1948; *Raleigh News and Observer*, November 17, 1948.
204. Ibid.
205. *Wilmington Star*, March 4, 1949; *Raleigh News and Observer*, March 4, 1949; Landon, *The North Carolina State Ports Authority*, 37–38. James T. Reside to Clyde R. Hoey, January 24, 1951, Clyde R. Hoey Papers, Manuscript Department, Perkins Library, Duke University, hereinafter cited as Hoey Papers; N.C. General Assembly Joint Resolution Number 20, 1949.

206.Quoted in Charles E. Landon, *The North Carolina State Ports Authority*, 7.
207. Landon, *The North Carolina State Ports Authority*, 7.
208. Ibid., 16–17.
209. Ibid., 9, 17.
210. *Wilmington Star*, February 26, 1946.
211. Ibid., May 9, 1946; *Raleigh News and Observer*, May 9, 1946.
212. *Wilmington Star*, May 9, 1946; *Raleigh News and Observer*, May 9, 1946.
213. W.W. Smith to R.B. Page, September 5, 1946, Cherry Papers.
214. *Wilmington Star*, October 9, 1946.
215. *Wilmington Star*, August 28, 1947; *Raleigh News and Observer*, August 28, 1947.
216. Ibid.
217. *Wilmington Star*, November 1, 1947.
218. *Wilmington Star*, February 26, 1948; March 30, 1948; *Raleigh News and Observer*, March 20, 1948; William W. Smith to Ronaldo B. Page, March 4, 1949, Hoey Papers.
219. *Wilmington Star*, June 16, 1948; U.S. Army Corps of Engineers, "Report on Cape Fear River, N.C.," Revised 1948, George W. Gillette Papers, Manuscript Department, Perkins Library, Duke University.
220. *Raleigh News and Observer*, March 4, 1949; Wilmington Chamber of Commerce to Frank Porter Graham, February 15, 1949, Frank Porter Graham papers, Southern Historical Collection, Wilson Library, University of North Carolina at Chapel Hill, hereinafter cited as Graham Papers; Cyrus D. Hogue to Clyde Hoey, February 8, 1949, Hoey Papers.
221. *Wilmington Star*, November 17, 1949; *Raleigh News and Observer*, November 17, 1949; George W. Gillette to Clyde R. Hoey, April 15, 1949, Hoey Papers.
222. Landon, *The North Carolina State Ports Authority*, 17–18.
223. *Wilmington Star*, November 17, 1949; *Raleigh News and Observer*, November 17, 1949; Landon, *The North Carolina State Ports Authority*, 17.

Bibliography

PRIMARY SOURCES

MANUSCRIPTS

Josiah Bailey Papers, Manuscript Department, Perkins Library, Duke University, Durham, North Carolina.

Graham Barden Papers, Manuscript Department, Perkins Library, Duke University, Durham, North Carolina.

George W. Gillette Papers, Manuscript Department, Perkins Library, Duke University, Durham, North Carolina.

Governors Papers, J. Melville Broughton, North Carolina State Archives, Raleigh, North Carolina.

Frank Porter Graham Papers, Southern Historical Collection, Wilson Library, University of North Carolina at Chapel Hill, North Carolina.

Industrial Union of Marine and Shipbuilding Workers of America Papers, Hornblake Library, University of Maryland, College Park Maryland.

National Labor Relations Board Records, Record Group 25, Federal Records Center, Suitland, Maryland.

New Hanover County (North Carolina) Court Records, New Hanover County Administrative Building, Wilmington, North Carolina.

North Carolina Department of Conservation and Development Papers, North Carolina State Archives, Raleigh, North Carolina.

North Carolina Shipbuilding Company Collection, East Carolina Manuscript Collection, Joyner Library, East Carolina University, Greenville, North Carolina.

North Carolina Shipbuilding Company Collection, Mariner's Museum Library, Newport News, Virginia.

State Ports Authority Minutes, North Carolina State Archives, Raleigh, North Carolina.

State Ports Authority, Records of the Morehead City Port Commission, North Carolina State Archives, Raleigh, North Carolina.

United States Army, Corp of Engineers Records, Record Group 77, Federal Records Center, Suitland, Maryland.

United States Executive Office of the President, Committee for Congested Production Areas Records, Record Group 212, Federal Records Center, Suitland, Maryland.

United States Maritime Commission Records, Record Group 178, National Archives, Washington, D.C.

United States Maritime Commission Records, Record Group 178, Federal Records Center, Suitland, Maryland.

United States Maritime Commission Records, Record Group 179, National Archives, Washington, D.C.

United States National Youth Administration Records, Record Group 119, Federal Records Center, Suitland, Maryland.

United States Navy, Office of the Coordinator of Ship Repair, Records, Record Group 45, National Archives, Washington, D.C.

United States Navy, Records of the Sixth (Charleston, South Carolina) Naval District, Record Group 181, Federal Records Center, East Point, Georgia.

United States Office of Community War Services, Record Group 215, National Archives, Washington, D.C.

United States War Labor Board Records, Record Group 202, Federal Records Center, Suitland, Maryland.

United States War Manpower Commission Records, Record Group 183, National Archives, Washington, D.C.

Wilmington, North Carolina City Council Records, Wilmington City Hall, Wilmington, North Carolina.

ORAL INTERVIEWS

Robert L. Burnett, Wilmington, North Carolina, February 23, 1978.

Percy F. Halsey, Newport News, Virginia, May 12, 1976.

J. Cargill Johnson, Newport News, Virginia, March 14, 1979.

William S. McMahon, Newport News, Virginia, April–May, 1976.

PRINTED GOVERNMENT DOCUMENTS

Chaikin, William. *Shipbuilding Policies of the War Production Board.* Washington, D.C.: Government Printing Office, 1947.

Fischer, Gerald J. *A Statistical Summary of Shipbuilding Under the U.S. Maritime Commission During World War II.* Washington, D.C.: Government Printing Office, 1949.

"North Carolina Shipbuilding Company. Industrial Union of Marine and Shipbuilding Workers of America." *National Labor Relations Board* 51, 251–56.

"North Carolina Shipbuilding Company vs. Industrial Union of Marine and Shipbuilding Workers of America." *National Labor Relations Board* 56, 1799–1804.

U.S. Bureau of Labor Statistics. *A Statistical Summary of the Wilmington Area; New Hanover County, North Carolina.* Washington, D.C.: Government Printing Office, 1943.

U.S. Bureau of Labor Statistics. *Wartime Employment, Production and Conditions of Work in Shipyards.* Washington, D.C.: Government Printing Office, 1945.

U.S. Maritime Administration. *Ships of America's Merchant Fleet.* Washington, D.C.: Government Printing Office, 1952.

U.S. Navy Secretary. *Final Report of a Board of Investigation to Inquire into the Design and Methods of Construction of Welded Steel Merchant Vessels.* Washington, D.C.: Government Printing Office, 1948.

U.S. Office of Production Management. *Ships for Freedom.* Washington, D.C.: Government Printing Office, 1944.

U.S. Senate. Special Committee Investigating the National Defense Program. *Hearings before…on January 12, March 2, 8, 27, 28, 30 and April 3, 1944, Part 23–Merchant Shipping.* Washington, D.C.: Government Printing Office, 1944.

NEWSPAPERS

Daily Press (Newport News, Virginia), 1941–1945.

News and Observer (Raleigh, North Carolina), 1942–1946.

North Carolina Shipbuilder (Wilmington, North Carolina), 1942–1946.

Shipyard Worker (Washington, D.C.), 1942–1946.

Star (Wilmington, North Carolina), 1942–1952.

SECONDARY SOURCES

MONOGRAPHS AND BIOGRAPHIES

Adams, Leonard. *Wartime Manpower Mobilization.* Ithaca: Cornell University Press, 1951.

Archibald, Katherine. *Wartime Shipyard.* Berkeley: University of California Press, 1947.

Baker, Laura Nelson. *Wanted: Women in War Industry: The Complete Guide to a War Factory Job.* New York: E.P. Dutton, 1943.

Benedetto, William R. *Sailing into the Abyss.* New York: Citadel Press, 2006.

Blewett, William E. *Always Good Ships: A History of the Newport News Shipbuilding and Dry Dock Company.* New York: Newcomen Society of the United States, 1960.

Blum, John Morton. *V Was for Victory.* New York : Harcourt Brace, 1976.

Brody, David. "Labor and the New Deal." In John Braeman, ed., *The New Deal and World War II.* Columbus : Ohio State University Press, 1975.

Brown, Alexander Crosby. *The Good Ships of Newport News; An Informal Account of Ships, An Informal Account of Shipping and Shipbuilding in the Chesapeake Bay.* Cambridge, MD: Tidewater Publications, 1976.

Bunker, John Gorley. *Liberty Ships: the Ugly Ducklings of World War II.* Annapolis: U.S. Naval Institute Press, 1972.

Campbell, Edward J. *A Century of Leadership: the History of the Newport News Shipbuilding and Dry Dock Company.* New York: Newcomen Society of the United States, 1986.

Carr, Lowell J. *Willow Run.* New York: Harper, 1952.

Clawson, Augusta H. *Shipyard Diary of a Woman Welder.* New York: Penguin Books, 1944.

Connery, Robert H. *The Navy and the Industrial Mobilization in World War II.* New York: DaCapo Press, 1972.

Course, A.G. *Deep Sea Tramp.* Barre, MA: Barre Publishing Co., 1963.

Dawson, Robert M. *The Conscription Crisis of 1944.* Toronto: University of Toronto Press, 1961.

Elphick, Peter. *Liberty: The Ships that Won the War.* Annapolis: Naval Institute Press, 2001.

Fassette, Frank G., Jr. *The Shipbuilding Business in the United States of America*. 2 vols. New York: The Society of Naval Architects and Marine Engineers, 1948.
Federal Writers Project. *North Carolina: A Guide to the Old North State*. Chapel Hill: University of North Carolina Press, 1939.
Fink, Gary M. *Labor Unions*. Westport, CT: Greenwood Press, 1977.
Finnie, Richard. *Marinship*. San Francisco: Marinship Corporation, 1947.
Five Years of North Carolina Shipbuilding. Wilmington: The North Carolina Shipbuilding Company, 1946.
Gripaios, Hector. *Tramp Shipping*. London: Thomas Nelson, 1959.
King, Spencer B., Jr. *The Selective Service in North Carolina in World War II*. Chapel Hill: University of North Carolina, 1949.
Land, Emory Scott. *Winning the War with Ships*. New York: McBride, 1958.
Landon, Charles E. *The North Carolina State Ports Authority*. Durham: Duke University Press, 1963.
Lane, Frederic C. *Ships for Victory*. Baltimore: Johns Hopkins University Press, 1951.
Massman, Emory A. *Hospital Ships of World War II*. Jefferson, N.C., McFarland & Co., 1999.
Mergen, Bernard. *A History of the Industrial Union of Marine and Shipbuilding Workers of America, 1933-1951*. Philadelphia: University of Pennsylvania Press, 1968.
Meyer, Agnes E. *Journey through Chaos*. New York : Harcourt Brace, 1943.
Moody's Manual of Investments: American and Foreign. New York: Moody's Investment Company, 1942–1948.
Moore, John R. *Senator Josiah William Bailey of North Carolina*. Durham: Duke University Press, 1968.
Nelson, Donald M. *Arsenal of Democracy*. New York: Harcourt, 1946.
North Carolina Shipbuilding Company. *By Laws of the North Carolina Shipbuilding Company*. Newport News: Newport News Shipbuilding and Dry Dock Company, 1941.
Novik, David. *Wartime Production Controls*. Urbana: University of Illinois Press, 1949.
Palmer, Mary Babcock. *We Fight With Merchant Ships*. Indianapolis: Bobbs-Merrill, 1943.
Pendleton, Ann. *Hit the Rivet, Sister*. New York: Howell, 1943.
Reeves, Bill. *Strength Through Struggle: The Chronological and Historical Record of the African-American Community in Wilmington, North Carolina, 1865–1950*. Wilmington, NC: New Hanover County Public Library, 1998.
Rupp, Leile. *Mobilizing Women for War*. Princeton: Princeton University Press, 1973.
Sawyer, L.A. *The Liberty Ships*. Cambridge, MD: Cornell Maritime Press, 1970.
———. *Victory Ships and Tankers*. Cambridge, MD: Cornell Maritime Press, 1974.
Steward, Ian G. *Liberty Ships in Peacetime*. Rockingham Beach, Western Australia, Ian Steward Marine Publications, 1992.
Tazwell, William L. *Newport News Shipbuilding: The First Century*. Newport News: Mariners' Museum, 1968.
Three Generations of Shipbuilding. Newport News, VA: Newport News Shipbuilding and Dry Dock Company, 1961.

Toulmin, Aubrey. *Diary of Democracy: The Senate War Investigating Committee*. New York: Richard Smith, 1947.
Von Miklos, Josephine. *I Took a War Job*. New York: Simon and Schuster, 1943.

ARTICLES

Blackman, John L. "Navy Policy Toward the Labor Relations of its War Contractors: Part One." *Military Affairs* 18 (Winter 1953), 176–87.
———. "Navy Policy Toward the Labor Relations of its War Contractors: Part Two." *Military Affairs* 19 (Spring 1955), 21–31.
Blum, Albert A. "Sailor or Worker : the Manpower Dilemma During the Second World War," *Labor History* 6 (Fall 1965), 232–47.
"The Deep South Looks up in Opportunity, With Northern Aid, to Join the Union." *Fortune* 28 (July 1943), 97–100, 218–25.
"Medicine: Voyage of the Vance," *Time*, June 3, 1946, 921–922.
Meyer, Henry C. "Some Design Problems of the Liberty Cargo Ships." *Journal of Engineering Education* 33 (January 1943), 454–62.
"Newport News Announces Plans to Build 25 of 200 Emergency Cargo Ships." *Marine Engineering and Shipbuilding Review* 6 (February 1941), 112.
"Newport News Shipbuilding and Dry Dock Company." *Fortune* 14 (November 1936), 68–75, 190.
Reed, Merl E. "The FEPC, the Black Worker and the Southern Shipyards," *South Atlantic Quarterly*, 74 (Autumn 1975), 446–60.
Rippy, J. Fred. "How the Wilmington, N.C., Water Department is Keeping up with the Demand," *American City* 59 (September 1944), 74–76.
"Shipbuilding at Wilmington." *The State* 12 (September 1944): 10–11, 16.
Society of Naval Architects and Marine Engineers. *Transactions*, XLVII (1949), 276.
Steiner, John W. "How to Light a Shipway." *Marine Engineering and Shipping Review*, 47 (May 1941), 175–77.
Wilkinson, Virginia. "From Housewife to Shipfitter." *Harper's* 187 (September 1943), 328–37.
"Wilmington Recreation Program." *American City* 59 (August 1944), 56.

All Photographs from North Carolina Shipbuilding Company Collection, East Carolina Manuscript Collection, Joyner Library, East Carolina University, Greenville, North Carolina.

The author would like to thank Dr. William N. Still of the East Carolina University History Department for first suggesting this line of research and for his encouragement and assistance.

Index

N

O

P

R

V

W

X

Y

Z